T0114516

Praise for
A Godward Heart

"As a longtime admirer of John Piper's powerful proclamation of the 'supreme-ness' of Christ in all things, I found this collection of short devotions to be comforting, thought provoking, and disturbing—all at the same time. Applying your understanding of the gospel to the real world has inescapable consequences. What you believe about the gospel determines the world you build. Here are, in a sense, John Piper's blueprints."

—KIRK CAMERON, actor, writer, producer

"Pastor John Piper has a way, through these devotions, of waking me up from spiritual slumber. God has used these meditations to open my eyes to truth that sets me free."

—SHANE BARNARD, recording artist

"My thirsty heart has often been directed to streams of living water through the devotional writings of Pastor John Piper. *A Godward Heart* is a fresh invitation to seek the Lord, to sit at the feet of the Savior, to savor Him as your greatest treasure, and to find deep satisfaction for your soul as you drink from His well that never runs dry."

—NANCY LEIGH DEMOSS, author, *Revive Our Hearts* teacher/host

A
GODWARD
HEART

Other Books by John Piper

Desiring God

The Pleasures of God

The Dangerous Duty of Delight

Finally Alive

Future Grace

A Hunger for God

Seeing and Savoring Jesus Christ

What's the Difference?

Don't Waste Your Life

When I Don't Desire God

Fifty Reasons Why Jesus Came to Die

God Is the Gospel

What Jesus Demands from the World

When the Darkness Will Not Lift

Spectacular Sins

John Calvin and His Passion for the Majesty of God

This Momentary Marriage

A Sweet and Bitter Providence

Think

Bloodlines

A GODWARD HEART

Treasuring the God Who Loves You

50 MEDITATIONS FOR YOUR JOURNEY

JOHN PIPER

Author of DESIRING GOD

MULTNOMAH

A Godward Heart

Scripture quotations are taken from The Holy Bible, English Standard Version, copyright © 2001 by Crossway Bibles, a division of Good News Publishers. Used by permission. All rights reserved. Scripture quotations marked (KJV) are taken from the King James Version. Scripture quotations marked (NASB) are taken from the New American Standard Bible®. © Copyright The Lockman Foundation 1960, 1962, 1963, 1968, 1971, 1972, 1973, 1975, 1977. Used by permission. (www.Lockman.org). Scripture quotations marked (NIV) are taken from the Holy Bible, New International Version®, NIV®. Copyright © 1973, 1978, 1984 by Biblica Inc.™ Used by permission of Zondervan. All rights reserved worldwide. www.zondervan.com.

Italics in Scripture quotations reflect the author's added emphasis.

Trade Paperback ISBN 978-0-593-19299-3
Hardcover ISBN 978-1-60142-566-9
eBook ISBN 978-1-60142-567-6

Copyright © 2014 by Desiring God Foundation

Cover design by Kristopher K. Orr; cover image by Robert McGouey, Corbis Images

Published in the United States by Multnomah, an imprint of Random House, a division of Penguin Random House LLC.

MULTNOMAH® and its mountain colophon are registered trademarks of Penguin Random House LLC.

The Library of Congress has cataloged the hardcover edition as follows:
Piper, John, 1946–
   A godward heart : treasuring the God who loves you / John Piper.—FIRST EDITION.
      pages cm
   ISBN 978-1-60142-566-9 (hardback)—ISBN 978-1-60142-567-6 (electronic)
   1. Meditations. I. Title.
   BV4832.3.P57 2014
   242—dc23

                                                  2013031510

CONTENTS

A WORD TO THE READER

One of the reasons I put together collections of short meditations is that my life has been changed as much by paragraphs as by books. Books on one topic are valuable. They let the author explore all the angles of an insight. But where do the insights themselves come from? Usually they come from paragraphs. Even sentences. For reasons not entirely explainable, God can make a single paragraph life changing.

Perhaps some evening your soul is hungry. Not for anything in particular, just a soul-hunger. A longing. Something is needed beyond what television is going to give. Something about God, or about the meaning of your life, or about eternity. You're tired and you know you probably can't stay awake to read twenty pages. So you pick up a book that you know focuses on eternal things, a Godward book. And three minutes later you have seen something, and you will never be the same again.

It may take a lifetime to sound the depths of what you just saw. But the seeing happens in an instant. It's as if God takes the paragraph in his fingers and uses it to adjust the lens on the eye of your soul, and something wonderful comes into focus that you had never seen before.

Isn't it amazing to think about the relationship between God's focusing fingers and the human activity of writing and reading? You may have read that same paragraph before, perhaps just the other evening. But this time God put his fingers on it and turned the lens just one more focusing notch. What this means is that I should pray as a writer and you should pray as a reader. We should ask God to do this focusing.

I think of your reading and my writing as a kind of partnership in the pursuit of a Godward miracle. I write, you read, but God gives the sight. What we both want is this miracle of seeing—seeing life-changing things about God and life and eternity.

In one of his letters the apostle Paul said, "*By reading* you can perceive my insight into the mystery of Christ" (Ephesians 3:4, author's translation). But was reading enough? A few sentences later he prayed that they "may have strength to...know the love of Christ" (Ephesians 3:18–19). Something more was needed than reading. Something from God—he called it "strength to know." Earlier he had prayed that the eyes of his readers' hearts would be "enlightened, that you may know" (Ephesians 1:18). Something from God is needed—in answer to prayer. This is what I meant when I said that God takes a human paragraph and puts his fingers on the lens of the eye of your soul. The slightest turn and we are made strong with sight. We are never the same again.

So I have written. And you are reading. And God is ready to act. My words are not Scripture. They are not infallible like God's words. But my earnest aim in all I write is to be faithful to God's written Word in the Bible. To point to God and his Son and his works and his ways. My aim is a Godward book in the hope that God will put his fingers on its paragraphs and turn the lens of the eye of your soul, ever so delicately, and bring glories into focus.

This is how God forms us into his image. "Beholding the glory of the Lord, [we] are being transformed into the same image from one degree of glory to another" (2 Corinthians 3:18). This is our aim: From a Godward paragraph, to a sight of glory, to *a Godward heart*.

❧

A very special word of thanks is due to David Mathis, executive editor at Desiring God. David helped me assemble these meditations from all the different places and times where I had written them. After I reworked them for this book, he provided his sharp theological, stylistic, and formatting eye to help me refine them for final release. I admire David's gifts and love his friendship. Thank you, David, for your partnership.

I have enjoyed a long and happy relationship with Multnomah Books, especially in bringing my shorter writings to publication. *A Godward Heart* is a continuation of what we began in *A Godward Life, Book One* (2001), continued in *A Godward Life, Book Two* (2003), *Pierced by the Word* (2003), *Life as a Vapor* (2004), and *Taste and See* (2005). I am thankful for this publishing partnership for the sake of spreading what I pray will prove to be life-changing, Christ-exalting paragraphs.

The Morning I Heard the Voice of God

When God's Word Gets Personal

Let me tell you about a most wonderful experience I had early Monday morning, March 19, 2007, a little after six o'clock. God actually spoke to me. There is no doubt that it was God. I heard the words in my head just as clearly as when a memory of a conversation passes across your consciousness. The words were in English, but they had about them an absolutely self-authenticating ring of truth. I know beyond the shadow of a doubt that God still speaks today.

I couldn't sleep for some reason. I was at Shalom House in northern Minnesota on a staff couples' retreat. It was about 5:30 in the morning. I lay there, wondering if I should get up or wait till I got sleepy again. In his mercy, God moved me out of bed. It was mostly dark, but I managed to find my clothing, get dressed, grab my briefcase, and slip out of the room without waking up Noël. In the main room below, it was totally quiet. No one else seemed to be up. So I sat down on a couch in the corner to pray.

As I prayed and mused, suddenly it happened. God said, *"Come and see what I have done."* There was not the slightest doubt in my mind that these were the very words of God, in this very moment. At this very place in the twenty-first century, 2007, God was speaking to me with absolute authority and self-evidencing reality. I paused to let this sink in. There was a sweetness about it. Time seemed to matter little. God was near. He had me in his sights. He had something to say to me. When God draws near, hurry ceases. Time slows down.

I wondered what he meant by "come and see." Would he take me somewhere, as he did Paul into heaven to see what can't be spoken? Did "see" mean that I would have a vision of some great deed of God that no one has seen? I am not sure how much time elapsed between God's initial word, *"Come and see what I have done,"* and his next words. It doesn't matter. I was being enveloped in the love of his personal communication. The God of the universe was speaking to me.

Then he said, as clearly as any words have ever come into my mind, *"I am awesome in my deeds toward the children of man."* My heart leaped up, "Yes, Lord! You are awesome in your deeds. Yes, to all men whether they see it or not. Yes! Now what will you show me?"

The words came again. Just as clear as before, but increasingly specific: *"I turned the sea into dry land; they passed through the river on foot. There they rejoiced in me, who rules by my might forever."* Suddenly I realized God was taking me back several thousand years to the time when he dried up the Red Sea and the Jordan River. I was being transported by his word back into history to those great deeds. This is what he meant by "come and see." He was transporting me back by his words to those two glorious deeds before the children of men. These were the "awesome deeds" he referred to. God himself was narrating the mighty works of God. He was doing it for me. He was doing it with words that were resounding in my own mind.

There settled over me a wonderful reverence. A palpable peace came down. This was a holy moment and a holy corner of the world in northern Minnesota. God Almighty had come down and was giving me the stillness and the openness and the willingness to hear his very voice. As I marveled at his power to dry the sea and the river, he spoke again. *"I keep watch over the nations—let not the rebellious exalt themselves."*

This was breathtaking. It was very serious. It was almost a rebuke, at least a warning. He may as well have taken me by the collar of my shirt, lifted me off the ground with one hand, and said with an incomparable mixture of fierceness and love, "Never, never, never exalt yourself. Never rebel against me."

I sat staring at nothing. My mind was full of the global glory of God. *"I keep watch over the nations."* He had said this to me. It was not just that he had said it. Yes, that is glorious. But he had said this to me. The very words of God were in my head. They were there in my head just as much as the words I am writing at this moment are in my head. They were heard as clearly as if at this moment I recalled that my wife said, "Come down for supper whenever you are ready." I know those are the words of my wife. And I know these are the words of God.

Think of it. Marvel at this. Stand in awe of this. The God who keeps watch over the nations, like some people keep watch over cattle or stock markets or construction sites—this God still speaks in the twenty-first century. I heard his very words. He spoke personally to me.

What effect did this have on me? It filled me with a fresh sense of God's reality. It assured me more deeply that he acts in history and in our time. It strengthened my faith that he is for me and cares about me and will use his global power to watch over me. Why else would he come and tell me these things?

It has increased my love for the Bible as God's very Word, because it was through the Bible that I heard these divine words, and through the Bible I have experiences like this almost every day. The very God of the universe speaks on every page into my mind—and your mind. We hear his very words. God himself has multiplied his wondrous deeds and thoughts toward us; none can compare with him! "I will proclaim and tell of them, yet they are more than can be told" (Psalm 40:5).

And best of all, they are available to all. If you would like to hear the very same words I heard on the couch in northern Minnesota, read Psalm 66:5–7. That is where I heard them. O how precious is the Bible. It is the very Word of God. In it God speaks in the twenty-first century. This is the very voice of God. By this voice, he speaks with absolute truth and personal force. By this voice, he reveals his all-surpassing beauty. By this voice, he reveals the deepest secrets of our hearts. No voice anywhere anytime can reach as deep or lift as high or carry as far as the voice of God that we hear in the Bible.

It is a great wonder that God still speaks today through the Bible with greater force and greater glory and greater assurance and greater sweetness and greater hope and greater guidance and greater transforming power and greater Christ-exalting truth than can be heard through any voice in any human soul on the planet from outside the Bible.

The great need of our time is for people to experience the living reality of God by hearing his word personally and "transformingly" in

Scripture. Something is incredibly wrong when words that claim to be from God from outside Scripture are more powerful and more affecting to us than the inspired Word of God.

Let us cry with the psalmist, "Incline my heart to your testimonies" (Psalm 119:36). "Open my eyes, that I may behold wondrous things out of your law" (Psalm 119:18). Grant that the eyes of our hearts would be enlightened to know our hope and our inheritance and the love of Christ that passes knowledge and be filled with all the fullness of God (Ephesians 1:18; 3:19). *O God, don't let us be so deaf to your Word and so unaffected with its ineffable, evidential excellency that we celebrate lesser things.*

What Does It Mean to Seek the Lord?

A Meditation on Psalm 105:4

"Seek the LORD and his strength;
seek his presence continually!"

—PSALM 105:4

Seeking the Lord means seeking his presence. *Presence* is a common translation of the Hebrew word for "face." Literally, we are to seek his face. But this is the Hebraic way of having access to God. To be before his face is to be in his presence.

But aren't his children always in his presence? Yes and no. Yes in two senses: First, it's yes in the sense that God is omnipresent and therefore always near everything and everyone. "He upholds the universe by the word of his power" (Hebrews 1:3). His power is ever present in sustaining and governing all things.

And second, yes, he is always present with his children in the sense of his covenant commitment to always stand by us and work for us and turn everything for our good. "Behold, I am with you always, to the end of the age" (Matthew 28:20). "I will never leave you nor forsake you" (Hebrews 13:5).

But there is a sense in which God's presence is not with us always. For this reason, the Bible repeatedly calls us to "seek the Lord...seek his presence continually." God's *manifest, conscious, trusted* presence is not our constant experience. There are seasons when we become neglectful of the Lord and give him no thought and do not put trust in him, and we find him "unmanifested"—that is, unperceived as great and beautiful and valuable by the eyes of our hearts.

His face—the brightness of his personal character—is hidden behind the curtain of our carnal desires. This condition is always ready to overtake us. That is why we are told to "seek his presence *continually.*" God calls us to enjoy continual consciousness of his supreme greatness and beauty and worth.

This happens through seeking. Continual seeking. But what does that mean practically? Both the Old and New Testaments say it means to set the mind and heart on God. It is the conscious fixing or focusing of our mind's attention and our heart's affection on God.

Now *set your mind and heart* to seek the Lord your God. (1 Chronicles 22:19)

If then you have been raised with Christ, *seek* the things that are above, where Christ is, seated at the right hand of God. *Set your minds* on things that are above, not on things that are on earth. (Colossians 3:1–2)

This setting of the mind is the opposite of mental coasting. It is a conscious choice to direct the heart toward God. That is what Paul prayed for the church: "May the Lord direct your hearts to the love of God and to the steadfastness of Christ" (2 Thessalonians 3:5). It is a conscious effort on our part. But that effort to seek God is a gift from God.

We do not make this mental and emotional effort to seek God because he is lost. That's why we would seek a coin or a sheep. But God is not lost. Nevertheless, there is always something through which or around which we must go to meet him consciously. This going through or around is what seeking is. He is often hidden. Veiled. We must go through mediators and around obstacles.

The heavens are telling the glory of God. So we can seek him through that. He reveals himself in his Word. So we can seek him through that. He shows himself to us in the evidences of grace in other people. So we can seek him through that. The seeking is the conscious effort to get through the natural means to God himself—to constantly set our minds toward God in all our experiences, to direct our minds and hearts toward him through the means of his revelation. This is what seeking God means.

And there are endless obstacles we must get around in order to see him clearly, and so that we can be in the light of his presence. We must flee every spiritually dulling activity. We must run from it and get around it. It is blocking our way.

We know what makes us vitally sensitive to God's appearances in the world and in the Word. And we know what dulls us and blinds us and makes us not even want to seek him. These things we must move away from and go around if we would see God. That is what seeking God involves.

And as we direct our minds and hearts Godward in all our experiences, we cry out to him. This too is what seeking him means.

"Seek the Lord while he may be found; *call* upon him while he is near" (Isaiah 55:6).

"Seek God and *plead* with the Almighty for mercy" (Job 8:5).

Seeking involves calling and pleading. *O Lord, open my eyes. O Lord, pull back the curtain of my own blindness. Lord, have mercy and reveal yourself. I long to see your face.*

The great obstacle to seeking the Lord is pride. "In the *pride* of his face the wicked does *not seek* him" (Psalm 10:4). Therefore, humility is essential to seeking the Lord.

The great promise to those who seek the Lord is that he will be found. "If you seek him, he will be found by you" (1 Chronicles 28:9). And when he is found, there is great reward. "Whoever would draw near to God must believe that he exists and that *he rewards those who seek him*" (Hebrews 11:6). God himself is our greatest reward. And when we have him, we have everything. Therefore, "Seek the Lord and his strength; seek his presence continually!"

Glorifying the Grace of God

Why Everything Exists

One of the main points of a short book I wrote, called *Spectacular Sins: And Their Global Purpose in the Glory of Christ* (Crossway, 2008), is that sin and God's wrath against it were part of God's plan when he created the world. This is different from saying that God sins or that he approves of sinning.

The main reason for making this point is to exalt the revelation of God's grace in the crucifixion of Jesus to the highest place. This is the point of the universe: the glorification of the grace of God in the apex of its expression in the death of Jesus.

Jesus died for sin (1 Corinthians 15:3). The death of Jesus for sin was planned before the foundation of the world. We know this because the book of Revelation refers to names written "before the foundation of the world in the book of life of the Lamb who was slain" (Revelation 13:8), and because Paul tells us that God saved us by "grace, which he gave us in Christ Jesus before the ages began" (2 Timothy 1:9).

Therefore, since Christ was slain for sin, and since grace is God's response to sin, we know that sin was part of the plan from the beginning. God carries this plan through in a way that maintains full human accountability, full hatred for sin, full divine justice, and full saving love for all who trust Christ. And we don't need to know *how* he does it to believe it and rest in it and worship him for it.

Recently I was pondering Ezra 8 and 9. I saw there another pointer to the truth of God's planning for human sin and divine wrath.

Ezra said, "The hand of our God is for good on all who seek him, and *the power of his wrath* is against all who *forsake him*" (Ezra 8:22). This text leads me to ask, did God know before creation that his creatures would "forsake him"? Yes, he did. The plan for their redemption was in place before the foundation of the world (Ephesians 1:3–6).

Was Ezra 8:22 true before the foundation of the world? Yes, it was. God did not become holy only after creation. He has always been holy and just. "The power of his wrath is against all who forsake him" because this is, and always has been, the holy and just thing for God to do.

Therefore, since God knew that his creatures would forsake him, he also knew that his power and wrath would be against them. Therefore, this was part of his plan. I'm not saying that fore*knowledge* is the same as pre*planning*. But I am saying that if God knew something would happen and he went ahead to put things in place that let it happen, then he does so for reasons. He does not act on a whim. And those reasons are what I mean by *plan*. He created the world knowing that sin would happen and that he would respond as Ezra 8:22 says he does. And thus he planned for it.

This planning is what Paul meant in Romans 9:22 when he said that God was "desiring to show his *wrath* and to make known his *power*." And if you ask Paul why God would go forward with this plan, his most ultimate answer is in the next verse: "In order to make known the riches of his glory for vessels of mercy" (Romans 9:23).

God knew that the revelation of his wrath and power against sin would make the riches of his glory shine all the brighter and taste all the sweeter for the vessels of mercy.

"The riches of his glory" are the riches we inherit when we see his glory in all the fullness that we can bear (Ephesians 1:18) and are transformed by it (Romans 8:30; 2 Corinthians 3:18; 1 John 3:2). These riches of glory reach their supreme height of wonder and beauty in the death of Jesus as he bore the condemnation of God's wrath and power in our place (Romans 8:3; Galatians 3:13).

In other words, God's plan that there be sin and wrath in the universe was ultimately to bring about "the praise of his glorious grace" in the death of Christ (Ephesians 1:6).

What is at stake in the sovereignty of God over sin is the ultimate aim of the universe, namely, the exaltation of the Son of God in the greatest act of wrath-removing, sin-forgiving, justice-vindicating grace that ever was or ever could be. The praise of the glory of God's grace in the death of Christ for sinners is the ultimate goal of all things.

This elevates Christ to the supreme place in the universe. When Paul said, "All things were created...for him" (Colossians 1:16), he meant that the entire universe and all the events in it serve to glorify Jesus Christ. And the apex of his glory is the glory of his grace, most clearly seen in his death for sinners like us.

O that God would make the meditations of our hearts go ever deeper into this mystery. And may the words of our mouths and the actions of our hands serve to magnify the infinite worth of Jesus and his death. This is why we exist.

How Is God's Passion for His Glory Not Selfishness?

God's Glory as the Source and Sum of Our Joy

The Bible is laden with God's self-exaltation. Repeatedly he says things like, "For my own sake, for my own sake, I do it, for how should my name be profaned? My glory I will not give to another" (Isaiah 48:11). A major question people have when they hear biblical texts about God's passion for his own glory is, how is this not a sinful form of narcissism and megalomania? The answer is, God's passion for his glory is the essence of his love to us. But narcissism and megalomania are not love.

God's love for us is not mainly his making much of us, but his giving us the ability to enjoy making much of him forever. In other words, God's love for us keeps God at the center. God's love for us exalts his value and our satisfaction in it. If God's love made us central and focused mainly on our value, it would distract us from what is most precious, namely, himself.

Love labors and suffers to enthrall us with what is infinitely and eternally satisfying: God. Therefore God's love labors and suffers to break our bondage to the idol of self and focus our affections on the treasure of God.

To see the God-centeredness of God's love demonstrated in Christ, look with me at the story of Lazarus's sickness and death:

> Now a certain man was ill, Lazarus of Bethany, the village of Mary and her sister Martha. It was Mary who anointed the Lord with ointment and wiped his feet with her hair, whose brother Lazarus was ill. So the sisters sent to him, saying, "Lord, he whom you love is ill." But when Jesus heard it he said, "This illness does not lead to death. It is for the glory of God, so that the Son of God may be glorified through it." Now Jesus loved Martha and her sister and Lazarus. So, [therefore] when he heard that Lazarus was ill, he stayed two days longer in the place where he was. (John 11:1–6)

Notice three amazing things:

1. Jesus chose to let Lazarus die. Verse 6 says, "When he heard that Lazarus was ill, he stayed two days longer in the place where he was." There was no hurry. His intention was not to spare the family grief but to raise Lazarus from the dead.

2. He was motivated by a passion for the glory of God displayed in his own glorious power. Verse 4 says, "This illness does not lead to death. It is for the glory of God, so that the Son of God may be glorified through it."

3. Nevertheless, both the decision to let Lazarus die and the motivation to magnify God were expressions of love for Mary and Martha and Lazarus. Verses 5–6 says, "Now Jesus loved Martha and her sister and Lazarus. So...he stayed...where he was."

O how many people today—even Christians—would murmur at Jesus for callously letting Lazarus die and putting him and Mary and Martha and others through the pain of those days. And if they saw that this was motivated by Jesus' desire to magnify the glory of God, many would call this harsh or unloving.

What this shows is how far above the glory of God most people value pain-free lives. For most people, love is whatever puts human value and human well-being at the center. So Jesus' behavior is scarcely intelligible to them.

But let us not tell Jesus what love is. Let us not instruct him how he should love us and make us central. Instead, let us learn from Jesus what love is and what our true well-being is.

Love is doing whatever you need to do, even to the point of dying on the cross, to help people see and savor the glory of God forever and ever. Love keeps God central, because the soul was made for God.

The mission statement of my life goes like this: *I exist to spread a passion for the supremacy of God in all things for the joy of all peoples through Jesus Christ.* People have asked me, *"Shouldn't love be part of it?"* My answer to those folks is, this mission statement *is* my definition of love.

Jesus confirms that we are on the right track here by the way he prays for us in John 17. I assume he is indeed praying for us because he says in verse 20, "I do not ask for these only, but also for those who will believe in me through their word." And I hope we would all agree that this prayer is an expression of his love for us (John 13:1). Consider how Jesus prays in the first five verses of John 17:

> When Jesus had spoken these words, he lifted up his eyes to heaven, and said, "Father, the hour has come; glorify your Son that the Son may glorify you, since you have given him authority over all flesh, to give eternal life to all whom you have given him. And this is eternal life, that they know you the only true God, and Jesus Christ whom you have sent. I glorified you on earth, having accomplished the work that you gave me to do. And now, Father, glorify me in your own presence with the glory that I had with you before the world existed" (vv. 1–5).

This is the way the Son of God prays when he is loving his people. He prays that his glory be upheld and displayed.

The connection with us comes in verse 24, "Father, I desire that they also, whom you have given me, may be with me where I am, to see my glory that you have given me because you loved me before the foundation of the world." The love of Jesus drives him to pray for us and then die for us, *not* that our value may be central, but that his glory may be central and that we may see it and savor it for all eternity. "To see my glory that you have given me"—for that, he let Lazarus die and for that he went to the cross.

The apostle Paul offered one illustration of God loving us this way:

> So to keep me from becoming conceited because of the surpassing greatness of the revelations, a thorn was given me

in the flesh, a messenger of Satan to harass me, to keep me
from becoming conceited. Three times I pleaded with the
Lord about this, that it should leave me. But he said to me,
"My grace is sufficient for you, for my power is made perfect in weakness." Therefore I will boast all the more gladly
of my weaknesses, so that the power of Christ may rest
upon me. For the sake of Christ, then, I am content with
weaknesses, insults, hardships, persecutions, and calamities. For when I am weak, then I am strong. (2 Corinthians
12:7–10)

Jesus' answer to Paul's plea that the painful thorn be removed was
no. The reason he gave to help Paul accept this answer was, "My
power is made perfect in weakness" (v. 9). In other words, he was saying it was more loving for him to help Paul value the glory of his
power than it was for him to take away his thorn.

Many less God-centered Christians, I fear, would not be happy
with that answer. I have heard Christians say, in so many words, "This
hurts and you can't be loving if you are going to subject me to this for
the rest of my life." In other words, God's love is defined as what
brings them the relief they want and makes them, not the glory of
Christ, central.

Paul's response was very different: "Therefore I will boast all the
more gladly of my weaknesses, so that the power of Christ may rest
upon me" (v. 9).

O how we need to see that Christ, not comfort, is our all-satisfying
and everlasting treasure. So I conclude that magnifying the supremacy of God in all things and being willing to suffer patiently to help

people see and savor this supremacy is the essence of love. It's the essence of God's love. And it's the essence of our love for people. Because the supremacy of God's glory is the source and sum of all full and lasting joy.

5

Galatians 4:18 and "Being Made Much Of"

Our Satisfaction in God's Supremacy

Galatians 4:18 seems to be in tension with what I often say about "being made much of." I ask, Do I feel more loved by God because he makes much of me, or because, at great cost to himself, he frees me to enjoy making much of him forever?

The point of that question is to expose the deepest foundation of our happiness. Is it God or me?

- Is the deepest basis of my joy God's greatness or my greatness?
- Am I more satisfied praising him or being praised?
- Am I God-centered because of his surpassing value, or am I God-centered because he highlights my surpassing value?
- Would it be heaven to me to see God or to be God?

In other words, the aim of that provocative question is not to deny that God does indeed make much of us in many ways, but rather to make sure he is kept supreme and central in his own love for us instead of making ourselves the supreme value in God's love.

In Galatians, Paul was warning the church that the Judaizers were seeking to win them over in subtle ways. He said, "They make much of you, but for no good purpose. They want to shut you out, that you may make much of them. It is always good to be made much of for a good purpose, and not only when I am present with you" (Galatians 4:17–18).

I am not happy with this translation of that passage, even though I am very happy with the overall translation of the English Standard Version. "Make much of" is not a close rendering of the Greek word *zeloō,* which usually carries the sense of "desire" or "long for" in a fairly strong way, either positively (zeal) or negatively (jealousy).

Here are three examples of the Greek word used as "bad desire," such as jealousy, envy, or covetousness:

- "And the patriarchs, jealous *(zēlōsantes)* of Joseph, sold him into Egypt; but God was with him" (Acts 7:9).
- "Love does not envy *(zēloi)* or boast" (1 Corinthians 13:4).
- "You desire and do not have, so you murder. You covet *(zēloute)* and cannot obtain, so you fight and quarrel" (James 4:2).

Here are two examples of the Greek word used as "good desire," like longing for, or proper jealousy, like God's:

- "Earnestly desire *(zēloute)* the higher gifts" (1 Corinthians 12:31).
- "For I feel a divine jealousy *(theou zelō)* for you, since I betrothed you to one husband, to present you as a pure virgin to Christ" (2 Corinthians 11:2).

In view of this meaning, the New American Standard Bible has, I think, a better translation of the Galatians passage: "They *eagerly seek* you, not commendably, but they wish to shut you out so that you will *seek* them. But it is good always to *be eagerly sought* in a commendable manner, and not only when I am present with you" (Galatians 4:17–18).

So the point of verse 18 is not that we should seek to be "made much of" but that we should act in such a way that, if we are eagerly sought out, it will be because our behavior is admirable. It is a good thing when people want to be around us or to imitate us because we follow Christ. "Be imitators of me, as I am of Christ" (1 Corinthians 11:1).

The aim is not to be made much of but to draw people into our passion for making much of Christ. So I don't think Galatians 4:17–18 is in tension with my question, "Do I feel more loved by God because he makes much of me, or because, at great cost to himself, he frees me to enjoy making much of him forever?" That question aims to accomplish the same thing as this text. It aims to make God's worth the supreme value in the universe and to show that his love for us is supremely his helping us be satisfied in that forever.

6

"I Love Jesus Christ"

An Unforgettable Moment in Seminary

One of the most memorable moments of my seminary days was during the school year 1968–69 at Fuller Seminary on the third level of the classroom building just after a class on systematic theology. A group of us were huddled around James Morgan, the young theology teacher who was saying something about the engagement of Christians in social justice. I don't remember what I said, but he looked me right in the eye and said, "John, I love Jesus Christ."

It was like a thunderclap in my heart. A strong, intelligent, mature, socially engaged man had just said out loud in front of a half-dozen men, "I love Jesus Christ." He was not preaching. He was not pronouncing on any issue. He was not singing in church. He was not trying to get a job. He was not being recorded. He was telling me that he loved Jesus.

The echo of that thunderclap is still sounding in my heart. That was forty-five years ago! There are a thousand things I don't remember about those days in seminary, but that afternoon remains unforgettable. And all he said was, "John, I love Jesus Christ."

James Morgan died a year later of stomach cancer, leaving a wife and four small children. His chief legacy in my life was one statement on an afternoon in Pasadena. "I love Jesus Christ."

Loving Jesus is natural and necessary for the children of God. It's natural because it's part of our nature as children of God. "If God were your Father, you would *love* me, for I came from God" (John 8:42). The children of God have the natural disposition to love his Son.

Loving Jesus is also necessary because Paul says that if you don't love Jesus, you will be cursed: "If anyone has no *love* for the Lord, let him be accursed" (1 Corinthians 16:22). Loving Jesus is an essential (not optional) mark of being a beneficiary of God's grace. "Grace be with all who *love* our Lord Jesus Christ with love incorruptible" (Ephesians 6:24). If you hold fast to the love of anything above Jesus, you are not his disciple: "Whoever loves father or mother more than me is not worthy of me, and whoever loves son or daughter more than me is not worthy of me" (Matthew 10:37).

Sometimes people reduce the meaning of love for Jesus to obedience. They quote John 14:15: "If you love me, you will keep my commandments." But that verse does *not* say keeping Jesus' commandments *is* love. It says that keeping his commandments *results* from love. "If you love me [that is the root], you will keep my commandments [that is the fruit]." And the root and the fruit are not the same. Love is something invisible and inside. It is the root that produces the visible fruit of loving others.

So I join James Morgan in saying, "I love Jesus Christ."

And as I say it, I want to make clear what I mean:

- I *admire* Jesus Christ more than any other human or angelic being.

- I *enjoy* his ways and his words more than I enjoy the ways and words of anyone else.
- I *want his approval* more than I want the approval of anyone else.
- I *want to be with him* more than I want to be with anyone else.
- I *feel more grateful* to him for what he has done for me than I do to anyone else.
- I *trust* his words more fully than I trust what anyone else says.
- I am *more glad in his exaltation* than in the exaltation of anyone else, including me.

Would you pray with me that we would love Jesus Christ more than we ever have? And may our Lord Jesus grant that from time to time we would deliver quietly and naturally a thunderclap into the hearts of others with the simple words, "I love Jesus Christ."

"Though you have not seen him, you love him. Though you do not now see him, you believe in him and rejoice with joy that is inexpressible and filled with glory" (1 Peter 1:8).

7

Every Step on the Calvary Road Was Love

The Intensity of Christ's Love and the Intentionality of His Death

The love of Christ for us in his dying was as conscious as his suffering was intentional. "By this we know love, that he laid down his life for us" (1 John 3:16). If he was intentional in laying down his life, the intention was for us. It was love to us. "When Jesus knew that his hour had come to depart out of this world to the Father, having loved his own who were in the world, he loved them to the end" (John 13:1). Every step on the Calvary road meant, "I love you."

Therefore, to feel the love of Christ in the laying down of his life, it helps to see how utterly intentional it was. Consider these five ways of seeing Christ's intentionality in dying for us.

First, look at what Jesus said just after that violent moment when Peter tried to cleave the skull of the servant but only cut off his ear.

Jesus said to Peter, "Put your sword back into its place. For all who take the sword will perish by the sword. Do you think that I cannot appeal to my Father, and he will at once send me more than twelve legions of angels? But how then should the Scriptures be fulfilled, that it must be so?" (Matthew 26:52–54).

It is one thing to say that the details of Jesus' death were predicted in the Old Testament. But it is much more to say that Jesus, in that night, himself was making his choices precisely to fulfill those Scriptures.

That is what Jesus said he was doing in Matthew 26:54. In effect he said, "I could escape this misery, but how then should the Scriptures be fulfilled, that it must be so? I am not choosing to take that way out because I know the Scriptures. I know what must take place. It is my choice to fulfill all that is predicted of me in the Word of God."

A second way the intentionality of his love for us is seen is in the repeated expressions of his intention to go to Jerusalem, into the very jaws of the lion.

Speaking to the Twelve as they traveled, Jesus said, "See, we are going up to Jerusalem, and the Son of Man will be delivered over to the chief priests and the scribes, and they will condemn him to death and deliver him over to the Gentiles. And they will mock him and spit on him, and flog him and kill him. And after three days he will rise" (Mark 10:33–34).

Jesus had a clear and all-controlling goal: to die according to the Scriptures. He knew when the time was near and set his face like flint: "When the days drew near for him to be taken up, he set his face to go to Jerusalem" (Luke 9:51).

A third way we see the intentionality of Jesus to suffer for us is in the words he spoke through the mouth of Isaiah the prophet: "I gave my back to those who strike, and my cheeks to those who pull out the beard; I hid not my face from disgrace and spitting" (Isaiah 50:6).

I have to work hard in my imagination to keep before me what iron will this required. Humans recoil from suffering. We recoil a hundred times more from suffering that is caused by unjust, ugly, sniveling, lowdown, arrogant people. At every moment of pain and indignity, Jesus chose not to do what would have been immediately just. He gave his back to the flogger. He gave his cheek to slapping. He gave his beard to plucking. He offered his face to spitting. And he was doing it for the very ones causing the pain. He was doing it intentionally for us.

A fourth way we see the intentionality of Jesus' suffering is in the way Peter explained how this was possible. He said, "When he was reviled, he did not revile in return; when he suffered, he did not threaten, but continued entrusting himself to him who judges justly" (1 Peter 2:23).

The way Jesus handled the injustice of it all was not by saying injustice doesn't matter, but by entrusting his cause to "him who judges justly." God would see that justice is done. That was not Jesus' calling at Calvary. Nor is it our highest calling now. "'Vengeance is mine, I will repay,' says the Lord" (Romans 12:19).

The fifth and perhaps the clearest statement that Jesus makes about his own intentionality to die is in John:

> For this reason the Father loves me, because I lay down my
> life that I may take it up again. No one takes it from me, but I
> lay it down of my own accord. I have authority to lay it down,
> and I have authority to take it up again. This charge I have
> received from my Father. (John 10:17–18)

Jesus' point in these words is that he is acting completely voluntarily. He is under no constraint from any mere human. Circumstances have not overtaken him. He is not being swept along in the injustice of the moment. He is in control.

Therefore, when John says, "By this we know love, that he laid down his life for us" (1 John 3:16), we should feel the intensity of his love for us to the degree that we see his intentionality to suffer and die. I pray that you will feel it profoundly. And may that profound experience of being loved by Christ have this effect on all of us: "The love of Christ controls us,…he died for all, that those who live might no longer live for themselves but for him who for their sake died and was raised" (2 Corinthians 5:14–15).

8

Be Careful, Lest the Light in You Be Darkness

Pondering a Puzzling Text

No one after lighting a lamp puts it in a cellar or under a basket, but on a stand, so that those who enter may see the light. Your eye is the lamp of your body. When your eye is healthy, your whole body is full of light, but when it is bad, your body is full of darkness. Therefore be careful lest the light in you be darkness. If then your whole body is full of light, having no part dark, it will be wholly bright, as when a lamp with its rays gives you light.

—Luke 11:33–36

Just before these verses, Jesus said, "Something greater than Solomon is here.... Something greater than Jonah is here" (Luke 11:31–32). That is, the wisdom of Jesus exceeds the greatest human wisdom, and the resurrection of Jesus will be greater than the most spectacular human rescues and resuscitations.

The question Jesus then addressed is, do we see this for what it is—magnificent and compelling—so it becomes the light and joy of our lives?

In the text above, Jesus talks about seeing, and he talks about two lamps. He said this about the first lamp: "No one after lighting a lamp puts it in a cellar or under a basket, but on a stand, so that those who enter may see the light" (v. 33).

I take this to refer to what Jesus had just said about his wisdom and resurrection. He set a lamp in the world—his wise and powerful presence—greater than Solomon and greater than Jonah. "I am the light of the world" (John 8:12; 9:5), he said. His greatness is the lamp that must not be hidden or missed.

He said this about the second lamp: "Your eye is the lamp of your body" (Luke 11:34).

I take this to mean that the way the lamp of Jesus becomes a lamp for you is that you see it for what it really is. Your eye becomes the lamp of your body when you see the lamp of his greatness in the world.

Then Jesus elaborated: "When your eye is healthy, your whole body is full of light, but when it is bad, your body is full of darkness" (v. 34). In other words, if your eye sees me for who I really am, then you are full of light; but if you don't see me for who I am, then you are full of darkness.

Then Jesus said, "Therefore be careful lest the light in you be darkness" (v. 35). In other words, there is much that passes for light through the eye that is not light. There are many bright things in the world that keep us from seeing the true light of Christ, just like city lights keep you from seeing the stars.

"Be careful!" he said. This is the only imperative in the text. Be careful what you see! Be careful what you regard as bright and attractive and compelling. If it is not Christ, you will be filled with darkness, no matter how bright it seems for a season. Candles seem bright until the sun comes out. Then they are useless and are put away.

Christ is the glory we were made to see. His light alone will fill us and give the light of life and meaning to every part of our lives. And when that happens, we ourselves will shine and give off the rays of Christ. "If then your whole body is full of light, having no part dark, it will be wholly bright, as when a lamp with its rays gives you light" (v. 36).

Lord, open the eyes of our hearts to see the supreme greatness of your wisdom and power. Make our eyes good. Heal our blindness. Fill us with the all-pervading, all-exposing, all-purifying, all-pleasing light of your presence.

9

Covering the Chasm

*The Rebellion of Nudity and
the Meaning of Clothing*

The first consequence of Adam's and Eve's sin was that "the eyes of both were opened, and they knew that they were naked. And they sewed fig leaves together and made themselves loincloths" (Genesis 3:7).

Suddenly they were self-conscious about their bodies. Before their rebellion against God, there was no shame. "The man and his wife were both naked and were not ashamed" (Genesis 2:25). Now there is shame. Why?

There is no reason to think it's because they suddenly became ugly. Their beauty wasn't the focus in Genesis 2:25, and their ugliness is not the focus in Genesis 3:7. Why then the shame? Because the foundation of covenant-keeping love collapsed. And with it the sweet, all-trusting security of marriage disappeared forever.

The foundation of covenant-keeping love between a man and a woman is the unbroken covenant between them and God—God governing them for their good, and they enjoying him in that security and relying on him. When they ate from the Tree of the Knowledge of Good and Evil, that covenant was broken and the foundation of their own covenant keeping collapsed.

They experienced this immediately in the corruption of their own covenant love for each other. It happened in two ways. Both relate to the experience of shame. In the first case, the spouse viewing my nakedness is no longer trustworthy, so I am afraid I will be shamed. In the second, I myself am no longer at peace with God, but I feel guilty and defiled and unworthy. I deserve to be shamed.

In the first case, I am self-conscious of my body, and I feel vulnerable to shame because I know Eve has chosen to be independent from God. She has made herself central in the place of God. She is essentially now a selfish person. From this day forward, she will put herself first.

She is no longer a servant. So she is not safe. And I feel vulnerable around her because she is very likely to put me down for her own sake. So suddenly my nakedness is precarious. I don't trust her anymore to love me with pure covenant-keeping love. That's one source of my fear and shame.

The other source is that Adam himself, not just his spouse, has broken covenant with God. If she is rebellious and selfish, and is therefore unsafe, so am I. But the way I experience it in myself is that I feel defiled and guilty and unworthy. That's, in fact, what I am. Before the Fall, what was and what ought to have been were the same. But now, what is and what ought to be are not the same.

I ought to be humbly and gladly submissive to God. But I am not. This huge gap between what I am and what I ought to be colors everything about me, including how I feel about my body. So my wife might be the safest person in the world, but now my own sense of guilt and unworthiness makes me feel vulnerable. The simple, open nakedness of innocence now feels inconsistent with the guilty person that I am. I feel ashamed.

So the shame of nakedness arises from two sources, and both of them are owing to the collapse of the foundation of covenant love in our relationship with God. One is that Eve is no longer reliable to cherish me; she has become selfish and I feel vulnerable that she will put me down for her own selfish ends. The other is that I already know that I am guilty myself, and the nakedness of innocence contradicts my unworthiness. I am ashamed of it.

Scripture says that they tried to cope with this new situation by making clothing: "They sewed fig leaves together and made themselves loincloths" (Genesis 3:7). Adam's and Eve's effort to clothe themselves was a sinful effort to conceal what had really happened. They tried to hide from God (Genesis 3:8). Their nakedness felt too revealing and too vulnerable. So they tried to close the gap between what they were and what they ought to be by covering what is, and presenting themselves in a new way.

So what does it mean that God clothed them with animal skins? Was he confirming their hypocrisy? Was he aiding and abetting their pretense? If they were naked and shame-free before the Fall, and if they put on clothes to minimize their shame after the Fall, then what was God doing by clothing them even better than they could clothe themselves? I think the answer is that he was giving a negative message and a positive message.

Negatively, he was saying, You are not what you were and you are not what you ought to be. The chasm between what you are and what you ought to be is huge. Covering yourself with clothing is a right response to this—not to conceal it, but to confess it. Henceforth, you shall wear clothing, not to conceal that you are not what you should be, but to confess that you are not what you should be.

One practical implication of this is that public nudity today is not a return to innocence but a rebellion against moral reality. God ordains clothes to witness to the glory we have lost, and it is added rebellion to throw them off.

And for those who rebel in the other direction and make clothes themselves a means of power and prestige and attention-getting, God's answer is not a return to nudity but a return to simplicity (1 Timothy 2:9–10; 1 Peter 3:4–5). Clothes are not meant to make people think about what is under them. Clothes are meant to direct attention to what is not under them: merciful hands that serve others in the name of Christ, beautiful feet that carry the gospel where it is needed, and a bright face that has beheld the glory of Jesus.

Now we have already crossed over to the more positive meaning of clothing that God had in his mind when he clothed Adam and Eve with animal skins. That was not only a witness to the glory we lost and a confession that we are not what we should be, but it is also a testimony that God himself would one day make us what we should be. God rejected their own self-clothing. Then he did it himself. He showed mercy with superior clothing.

Together with the other hopeful signs in the context (like the defeat of the serpent in Genesis 3:15), God's mercy points to the day when he will solve the problem of our shame decisively and permanently. He will do it with the blood of his own Son (as there apparently was bloodshed in the killing of the animals of the skins). And he will do it with the clothing of righteousness and the radiance of his glory (Galatians 3:27; Philippians 3:9, 21).

Which means that our clothes are a witness both to our past and present failure *and* to our future glory. They testify to the chasm between what we are and what we should be. And they testify to God's merciful intention to bridge that chasm through Jesus Christ and his death for our sins.

10

Discerning Idolatry in Desire

Twelve Ways to Recognize the Rise of Covetousness

Most of us realize that enjoying anything other than God, from the best gift to the basest pleasure, can become idolatry. Paul said that covetousness is idolatry (Colossians 3:5). Covetousness means "desiring something other than God in the wrong way." But what does "in the wrong way" mean?

The reason this matters is both vertical and horizontal. Idolatry will destroy our relationship with God. And it will also destroy our relationships with people.

All human relational problems—from marriage and family to friendship to neighbors to classmates to colleagues—are rooted in various forms of idolatry, that is, wanting things other than God in wrong ways.

So here is my effort to think biblically about what those wrong ways are. What makes an enjoyment idolatrous? What turns a desire into covetousness, which is idolatry?

1. *Enjoyment is becoming idolatrous when it is forbidden by God.* For example, adultery and fornication and stealing and lying are forbidden by God. Some people, at times, feel that these are pleasurable, or else they would not do them. No one sins out of duty. But such pleasure is a sign of idolatry.

2. *Enjoyment is becoming idolatrous when it is disproportionate to the worth of what is desired.* Great desire for nongreat things is a sign that we are beginning to make those things idols.

3. *Enjoyment is becoming idolatrous when it is not permeated with gratitude.* When our enjoyment of something tends to make us not think of God, it is moving toward idolatry. But if the enjoyment gives rise to the feeling of gratefulness to God, we are being protected from idolatry. The grateful feeling that we don't deserve this gift or this enjoyment, but have it freely from God's grace, is evidence that idolatry is being checked.

4. *Enjoyment is becoming idolatrous when it does not see in God's gift that God himself is to be desired more than the gift.* If the gift is not awakening a sense that God, the Giver, is better than the gift, it is becoming an idol.

5. *Enjoyment is becoming idolatrous when it is starting to feel like a right, and our delight is becoming a demand.* It may be that the delight is right. It may be that another person ought to give you this delight. It may be right to tell them this. But when all this rises to the level of angry demands or self-pitying resentment, idolatry is rising.

6. *Enjoyment is becoming idolatrous when it draws us away from our duties.* When we find ourselves spending time

pursuing an enjoyment, knowing that other things or
people should be getting our attention, we are moving into
idolatry.

7. *Enjoyment is becoming idolatrous when it awakens a sense
of pride that we can experience this delight while others can't.*
This is especially true of delights in religious things, like
prayer and Bible reading and ministry. It is wonderful to
enjoy holy things. It is idolatrous to feel proud that we can.

8. *Enjoyment is becoming idolatrous when it is oblivious or callous
to the needs and desires of others.* Holy enjoyment is aware of
others' needs and may temporarily leave a good pleasure to
help another person have it. One might leave private prayer
to be the answer to someone else's.

9. *Enjoyment is becoming idolatrous when it does not desire that
Christ be magnified as supremely desirable through the enjoyment.* Enjoying anything but Christ (like his good gifts)
runs the inevitable risk of magnifying the gift over the
Giver. One evidence that idolatry is not happening is the
earnest desire that this not happen.

10. *Enjoyment is becoming idolatrous when it is not working a
deeper capacity for holy delight.* We are sinners still. It is idolatrous to be content with sin. So we desire transformation.
Some enjoyments shrink our capacities of holy joy. Others
enlarge them. Some go either way, depending on how we
think about them. When we don't care if an enjoyment is
making us more holy, we are moving into idolatry.

11. *Enjoyment is becoming idolatrous when its loss ruins our
trust in the goodness of God.* There *can* be sorrow at loss

without being idolatrous. But when the sorrow threatens our confidence in God, it signals that the thing lost was becoming an idol.

12. *Enjoyment is becoming idolatrous when its loss paralyzes us emotionally so that we can't relate lovingly to other people.* This is the horizontal effect of losing confidence in God. Again, great sorrow is no sure sign of idolatry. Jesus had great sorrow. But when desire is denied, and the effect is the emotional inability to do what God calls us to do, the warning lights of idolatry are flashing.

For myself and for you, I pray the admonition of John: "Little children, keep yourselves from idols" (1 John 5:21).

11

The Precious Gift of Baby Talk

Human Language as the Precious Path to Knowing God

Human language is precious. It sets us apart from animals. It makes our most sophisticated scientific discoveries and our deepest emotions sharable. Above all, God chose to reveal himself to us through human language in the Bible.

At the fullness of time, he spoke to us by a Son (Hebrews 1:1–2). That Son spoke human language, and he sent his Spirit to lead his apostles into all truth so they could tell the story of the Son in human language. Without this story in human language, we would not know the Son. Therefore, human language is immeasurably precious.

But it is also imperfect for capturing the fullness of God. In 1 Corinthians 13, there are four comparisons between this present time and the age to come after Christ returns.

Love never ends. As for prophecies, they will pass away; as for tongues, they will cease; as for knowledge, it will pass away.

For we know in part and we prophesy in part, but when the perfect comes, the partial will pass away. When I was a child, I spoke like a child, I thought like a child, I reasoned like a child. When I became a man, I gave up childish ways. For now we see in a mirror dimly, but then face to face. Now I know in part; then I shall know fully, even as I have been fully known. So now faith, hope, and love abide, these three; but the greatest of these is love. (1 Corinthians 13:8–13)

Note the comparisons with this age (now) and the age to come (then):

> Now: We know in part.
> Then: When the perfect comes, the partial will pass
>   away (vv. 9–10).

> Now: I spoke and thought and reasoned like a child.
> Then: When I became a man, I gave up childish
>   ways (v. 11).

> Now: We see in a mirror dimly.
> Then: We will see face to face (v. 12).

> Now: I know in part.
> Then: I will know fully, even as I am fully known (v. 12).

In this context, we can see what Paul meant by saying, "When I was a child, I spoke like a child, I thought like a child, I reasoned like a child." He was saying that in this age, our human language and thought and reasoning are like baby talk compared to how we will speak and think and reason in the age to come.

When Paul was caught up into heaven and given glimpses of heavenly realities, he said he "heard things that cannot be told, which man may not utter" (2 Corinthians 12:4). Our language is insufficient to carry the greatness of all that God is.

But what a blunder it would be to infer from this that we may despise language or treat it with contempt or carelessness. What a blunder, if we began to belittle true statements about God as cheap or unhelpful or false. What folly it would be if we scorned prepositions and clauses and phrases and words, as though they were not inexpressibly precious and essential to life.

The main reason this would be folly is that God has chosen to send his Son into our nursery and speak baby talk with us. Jesus Christ became a child with us. There was a time when Jesus himself would have said, "When I was a child, I spoke like a child and thought like a child and reasoned like a child." That is what happened in the Incarnation. He accommodated himself to our baby talk. He stammered with us in the nursery of human life in this age.

Jesus spoke baby talk. The Sermon on the Mount is our baby talk. His high priestly prayer in John 17 is baby talk. "My God, My God, why have you forsaken me?" (Matthew 27:46; Mark 15:34) is baby talk. He spoke infinitely precious, true, glorious baby talk.

More than that, God inspired an entire Bible of baby talk. True baby talk. Infallible baby talk. Baby talk with absolute authority and power. Baby talk that is sweeter than honey and more to be desired than gold (see Psalm 19:10). John Calvin said that "God, in so

speaking, lisps with us as nurses are wont to do with little children."*
O, how precious is the baby talk of God. It is not like grass that with-
ers or flowers that fade. It stands forever (Isaiah 40:8).

There will be another language and thought and reasoning in the
age to come. And we will see things that could not have been expressed in our present baby talk. But when God sent his Son into our
human nursery, talking baby talk and dying for the toddlers, he shut
the mouths of those who ridicule the possibilities of truth and beauty
in the mouth of babes.

And when God inspired a book with baby talk as the infallible
interpretation of himself, what shall we say of the children who make
light of the gift of human language as the medium of knowing God?
Woe to those who despise or belittle or exploit or manipulate this gift
to the children of man. It is not a toy in the nursery. It is the breath of
life. "The words that I have spoken to you are spirit and life" (John
6:63).

---

*John Calvin, *Institutes of the Christian Religion,* originally published 1536, 1.13.1.

12

Let Christians Vote as Though Not Voting

*Political Engagement When
the World Is Passing Away*

Voting is like marrying and crying and laughing and buying. We should do it, but only as if we were not doing it. That's because "the present form of this world is passing away" and, in God's eyes, "the time has grown very short." Here's the way Paul put it:

> The appointed time has grown very short. From now on, let those who have wives live as though they had none, and those who mourn as though they were not mourning, and those who rejoice as though they were not rejoicing, and those who buy as though they had no goods, and those who deal with the world as though they had no dealings with it. For the present form of this world is passing away. (1 Corinthians 7:29–31)

Let's take these points one at a time and compare them to voting.

1. "Let those who have wives live as though they had none" (v. 29).

This doesn't mean move out of the house, don't have sex, and don't call her "Honey." Earlier in this chapter Paul said, "The husband should give to his wife her conjugal rights" (1 Corinthians 7:3). He also said to love her the way Christ loved the church, leading and providing and protecting (Ephesians 5:25–30). What it means is that marriage is momentary. It's over at death, and there is no marriage in the resurrection. Wives and husbands are second priorities, not first. Christ is first. Marriage is for making much of him.

So that means if she is exquisitely desirable, beware of desiring her more than Christ. And if she is deeply disappointing, beware of being hurt too much. This is temporary—only a brief lifetime. Then comes the never-disappointing life that is life indeed.

So it is with voting. We should do it, but only as if we were not doing it. Its outcomes do not give us the greatest joy when they go our way, and they do not demoralize us when they don't. Political life is for making much of Christ, whether the world falls apart or holds together.

2. "And those who mourn [do so] as though they were not mourning" (v. 30).

Christians mourn with real, deep, painful mourning, especially over losses—loss of those we love, loss of health, loss of a dream. These losses hurt. We cry when we are hurt. But we cry as though not crying. We mourn knowing we have not lost something so valuable we cannot rejoice in our mourning. Our losses do not incapacitate us. They do not blind us to the possibility of a fruitful future serving

Christ. The Lord gives and takes away, but he remains blessed (Job 1:21). And we remain hopeful in our mourning.

So it is with voting. There are losses. We mourn. But not as those who have no hope. We vote and we lose, or we vote and we win. In either case, we win or lose as if we were not winning or losing. Our expectations and frustrations are modest. The best this world can offer is short and small. The worst it can offer has been predicted in the book of Revelation. And no vote will hold it back. In the short run, Christians lose (Revelation 13:7). In the long run, we win (Revelation 21:4).

3. "And those who rejoice [do so] as though they were not rejoicing" (v. 30).

Christians rejoice in health (James 5:13) and in sickness (James 1:2). There are a thousand good things that come down from God that call forth the feeling of happiness. Beautiful weather. Good friends who want to spend time with us. Delicious food and someone to share it with. A successful plan. A person helped by our efforts.

But none of these good and beautiful things can satisfy our soul. Even the best cannot replace what we were made for, namely, the full experience of the risen Christ (John 17:24). Even fellowship with him here is not the final and best gift. There is more of him to have after we die (Philippians 1:21–23), and even more after the resurrection (2 Corinthians 5:1–5). The best experiences here are foretastes. The best sights of glory are through a mirror dimly. The joy that rises from these previews does not and should not rise to the level of the hope of glory. These pleasures will one day be as though they were not.

So we rejoice remembering this joy is a foretaste and will be replaced by a vastly better joy. Not less. And not less material. But better in the radically renewed material universe. God created matter and will not simply throw it away. He will not turn the whole universe into a spirit. But in that new material universe with a resurrected, material body, which Paul nevertheless called a "spiritual body" (1 Corinthians 15:44), our joy will be vastly superior to all we have known here.

So it is with voting. There are joys. The very act of voting is a joyful statement that we are not under a tyrant. And there may be happy victories. But the best government we get is a foreshadowing. Peace and justice are approximated now. They will be perfect when Christ comes. So our joy is modest. Our triumphs are short lived—and shot through with imperfection. So we vote as though not voting.

4. *"And those who buy [do so] as though they had no goods"* *(v. 30).*

Let Christians keep on buying while this age lasts. Christianity is not withdrawal from business. We are involved but as though not involved. Business simply does not have the weight in our hearts that it has for many. All our getting and all our having in this world are getting and having things that are not ultimately important. Our car, our house, our books, our computers, our heirlooms—we possess them with a loose grip. If they are taken away, we say that, in a sense, we did not have them. We are not here to possess. We are here to lay up treasures in heaven (Matthew 6:19–20).

This world matters, but it is not ultimate. It is the stage for living in such a way as to show that this world is not our God but that Christ is our God. It is the stage for using the world to show that Christ is more precious than the world.

So it is with voting. We do not withdraw. We are involved, but as if not involved. Politics does not have ultimate weight for us. It is one more stage for acting out the truth that Christ, and not politics, is supreme.

5. *"And those who deal with the world [do so] as though they had no dealings with it" (v. 31).*

Christians should deal with the world. This world is here to be used. Dealt with. There is no avoiding it. Not to deal with it is to deal with it that way. Not to weed your garden is to cultivate a weedy garden. Not to wear a coat in Minnesota is to freeze, to deal with the cold that way. Not to stop when the light is red is to spend your money on fines or hospital bills or lawsuits or a funeral and deal with the world that way. We must deal with the world.

But as we deal with it, we don't give it our fullest attention. We don't ascribe to the world the greatest status. There are unseen things that are vastly more precious than the world. We use the world without offering it our whole soul. We may work with all our might when dealing with the world, but the full passions of our heart will be attached to something higher—Godward purposes. We use the world but not as an end in itself. It is a means. We deal with the world as a gratefully received gift *from* Christ and in order to make much *of* Christ.

So it is with voting. We deal with the system. We deal with the news. We deal with the candidates. We deal with the issues. But we deal with it all as if not dealing with it. It does not have our fullest attention. It is not the great thing in our lives. Christ is. And Christ will be ruling over his people with perfect supremacy, no matter who is elected and no matter what government stands or falls. So we vote as though not voting.

By all means vote. But remember, "The world is passing away along with its desires, but whoever does the will of God abides forever" (1 John 2:17).

13

Does God Lie?

*Reflections on God's Truthfulness
and Sovereignty over Falsehood*

oes God lie? The short answer is no. God never says anything like "I am not God." Or "You are not sinful." Or "Christ is not a great Savior." Or "If you believe in Christ, you will not be saved." Or "It is foolish to follow my counsel." Or "My word is unreliable."

But God does ordain that lying happens as part of his judgment on the guilty. That is why the question comes up.

- The prophet Micaiah stood against all the prophets of Ahab and said that the king would fall in battle. To explain why all the other prophets were saying the opposite, Micaiah said, "Now therefore behold, *the LORD has put a lying spirit in the mouth of all these your prophets;* the LORD has declared disaster for you" (1 Kings 22:23).

- Similarly, God said he will punish those who try to use prophets to buttress their sin. In that situation he said, "If the prophet is deceived and speaks a word, *I, the LORD, have deceived that prophet,* and I will stretch out

my hand against him and will destroy him from the
midst of my people Israel. And they shall bear their punishment—the punishment of the prophet and the punishment of the inquirer shall be alike" (Ezekiel 14:9–10).

- And at the end of this age, God will ordain a "strong delusion" as part of the punishment for those who "refused
to love the truth":

The coming of the lawless one is by the activity of Satan with
all power and false signs and wonders, and with all wicked
deception for those who are perishing, because they refused
to love the truth and so be saved. Therefore *God sends them a
strong delusion,* so that they may believe what is false, in order
that all may be condemned who did not believe the truth but
had pleasure in unrighteousness. (2 Thessalonians 2:9–12)

When we say that God never lies, but ordains that lying happens,
we do not mean that he approves of lying or that his law permits lying.
We mean that God governs all things in the universe, including the
sins of sinful men. Sin does not cease to be sin because God governs it
and guides it for the good of his people and the glory of his name.

That is what he did in the sin of Joseph's brothers' deceptive sale
of him into Egypt (Genesis 50:20) and Judas's deceptive kiss of be-
trayal (Luke 22:2–22; Acts 2:23). The one led to the greatest act of
salvation in the Old Testament (the Exodus from Egypt), and the
other led to the greatest act of salvation in history (the death of Christ
for our sins).

When God said, "I, the LORD, have deceived that prophet"

(Ezekiel 14:9), he meant that he can and does govern a sinful prophet's mind so that the prophet believes a lie. But God does it in such a way that he himself is not lying. God is able to superintend a thousand circumstances and influences so that a sinful prophet will think a lie, without God himself lying or in any way compromising his perfect truthfulness.

Let the Word of God about the word of God stand firm:

- "God is not man, that he should lie, or a son of man, that he should change his mind. Has he said, and will he not do it? Or has he spoken, and will he not fulfill it?" (Numbers 23:19).
- "The Glory of Israel will not lie" (1 Samuel 15:29).
- "The word of the LORD is upright, and all his work is done in faithfulness" (Psalm 33:4).
- "This God—his way is perfect; the word of the LORD proves true" (2 Samuel 22:31).
- "Every word of God proves true" (Proverbs 30:5).
- "The words of the LORD are pure words, like silver refined in a furnace on the ground, purified seven times" (Psalm 12:6).

God can be trusted. But do not play games with him. Do not begin to be careless with the truth. Do not take "pleasure in unrighteousness" and forsake the love of the truth. If you do, you may be abandoned to "a strong delusion" and never be able to see again (2 Thessalonians 2:10–12). God's elect will never be abandoned to apostasy, for he keeps his elect in the truth (Hebrews 13:21).

14

When Satan Hurts Christ's People

*Reflections on Why
Christians Suffer Losses*

When huge pain comes into your life—such as divorce, or the loss of a precious family member, or the shattered dream of wholeness—it is good to have a few things settled with God ahead of time. The reason for this is not because it makes grieving easy, but because it gives focus and boundaries for the pain.

Being confident in God does not make the pain less deep but less broad. If some things are settled with God, there are boundaries around the field of pain. In fact, by being focused and bounded, the pain of loss may go deeper, as a river with banks runs deeper than a flood plain. But with God in his firm and proper place, the pain need not spread out into the endless spaces of ultimate meaning. This is a great blessing, though at the time it may simply feel no more tender than a brick wall. But what a precious wall it is!

As a father, I wanted to help our twelve-year-old daughter Talitha settle some things with God then, so that when little or big losses come—and I knew they would come, and will come—her pain would be bounded and would not carry her out like a riptide into the terrifying darkness of doubt about God. So as we would read God's Word together twice a day, I pointed out the mysterious ways of God.

So one day we read this from the lips of Jesus to the church at Smyrna:

> Do not fear what you are about to suffer. Behold, the devil is about to throw some of you into prison, that you may be tested, and for ten days you will have tribulation. Be faithful unto death, and I will give you the crown of life. (Revelation 2:10)

I asked Talitha, "Is Jesus stronger than the devil?"

"Yes," she said.

"Indeed," I added, "ten million times stronger. It's not even close. In fact, as Mark 1:27 says, 'He commands even the unclean spirits, and they obey him.' So all Jesus has to do is say to the devil, 'You shall not throw my loved ones into prison,' and the devil will not be able to do it. Right, Talitha?"

"Right," she said.

"So, Talitha, why does Jesus let the devil do this? Why does he let the devil throw his precious followers in jail and even kill some of them?" She shook her head. I said, "Well, let's read it again slowly, and you tell me the reason that the Bible gives. 'Behold the devil is about to throw some of you into prison…that…you…may…be…tested.' So why does Jesus let this happen, Talitha?"

"That they may be tested."

"That's right. And what does it mean to be tested? The answer is given in the way Jesus described what passing the test looks like. He said, 'Be faithful unto death, and I will give you the crown of life.' Faithfulness to Jesus is being tested. Will his loved ones keep trusting him? Will they keep believing that he has their best interest at heart? That he is wise? That he is good? That he is stronger than all?

"So, Talitha, there are a thousand things that God is doing every time something painful happens to you. Most of these you do not know or understand. Job, Joseph, and Esther didn't know what God was doing in their losses—not when the losses were happening. But there is always one thing you *can* know God is doing when pain comes into your life. This is something you can settle with God ahead of time. He is always testing you.

"If the test leads to your death, as it did for some of the Christians in Smyrna, Jesus wants you to know something ahead of time. You will receive 'the crown of life.' That means he will raise you from the dead and will crown you with the kind of everlasting joy in his presence that will make up for your losses ten thousandfold. *Crown* signifies 'majestic, royal restoration, and exaltation.'

"James says the same thing: 'Blessed is the man who remains steadfast under trial, for when he has stood the test he will receive the crown of life, which God has promised to those who love him' (James 1:12).

"Passing the test means loving God to the end. So settle it, Talitha. Loss and pain will come into your life. But Jesus is infinitely stronger than the devil. So even if the devil is causing it, as he did in Smyrna, Jesus is letting it happen. He's still in control. And he always has his reasons for what he permits—more reasons than we can know. One of those reasons is always testing, namely, the testing of our faith and our love for him."

We cannot answer every *why* question. But there is always this answer: my faith is being tested by the Lord who loves me and will help me. And our Lord never wastes his tests. Whether we believe this truth is, in fact, part of the test. In the mind of Jesus, the promise that he would give them the crown of life was enough to sustain the Christians in Smyrna. I praise God that this has been, and pray that it always will be enough for Talitha—and for you.

15 ~

Apostle of Jesus and Abolitionist with the Gospel

How Paul Worked to Overcome Slavery

The historic and contemporary reality of slavery is never far away from how we think about the Bible. Instead of a frontal attack on the culturally pervasive institution of slavery in his day, Paul took another approach, for example, in his letter to Philemon.

Onesimus was a slave. His master, Philemon, was a Christian. Onesimus had evidently run away from Colossae (Colossians 4:9) to Rome where Paul, in prison, had led him to faith in Jesus—an amazing providence, since Paul evidently knew Onesimus's master. Now he was sending Onesimus back to Philemon. This letter tells Philemon how to receive Onesimus.

In the process, Paul did at least eleven things that work together to undermine slavery.

1. Paul drew attention to Philemon's love for all the saints: "I hear of your love and of the faith that you have toward the Lord Jesus and for all the saints" (Philemon 1:5). This puts

Philemon's relation with Onesimus (now one of the saints) under the banner of love, not just commerce.

2. Paul modeled for Philemon the superiority of appeals over commands when it comes to relationships governed by love: "Accordingly, though I am bold enough in Christ to command you to do what is required, yet for love's sake I prefer to appeal to you" (vv. 8–9). This points Philemon to the new dynamics that will hold sway between him and Onesimus. Acting out of freedom from a heart of love is the goal in the relationship.

3. Paul heightened the sense of Onesimus's being in the family of God by calling him his child: "I appeal to you for my child, Onesimus, whose father I became in my imprisonment" (v. 10). Remember, Philemon, however you deal with him, you are dealing with my child.

4. Paul raised the stakes again by saying that Onesimus had become woven into Paul's own deep affections: "I am sending him back to you, sending my very heart" (v. 12). The word for *heart* is "bowels." So he was saying, "I am deeply bound emotionally to this man, so treat him that way."

5. Paul again emphasized that he wanted to avoid force or coercion in his relationship with Philemon: "I would have been glad to keep him with me...but I preferred to do nothing without your *consent* in order that your goodness might not be by compulsion but of your own accord" (vv. 13–14). He was instructing Philemon how to deal with Onesimus so he too would act "of his own accord."

6. Paul raised the intensity of the relationship again with the word *forever* when he said, "This perhaps is why he was parted from you for a while, that you might have him back forever" (v. 15). In other words, Onesimus would not be coming back into any ordinary, secular relationship but a forever relationship.

7. Paul said that Philemon's relationship would no longer be the usual master-slave relationship: "[You have him back] *no longer as a slave* but more than a slave, as a beloved brother" (v. 16). Whether Philemon would let Onesimus go back as a free man to serve Paul or keep him in his service, things could not remain as they were. "No longer as a slave" did not lose its force when Paul added "more than a slave."

8. In that same verse (v. 16), Paul referred to Onesimus as Philemon's "beloved brother." This is the relationship that takes the place of slave. "No longer as a slave but…as a beloved brother." Onesimus got the "holy kiss" (1 Thessalonians 5:26) from Philemon and would eat by his side at the Lord's Table.

9. Paul made clear that Onesimus was with Philemon in the Lord: "[He is] a beloved brother…in the Lord" (Philemon 1:16). Onesimus's identity was now the same as Philemon's. He was "in the Lord." Union with Christ is the great barrier-demolishing reality.

10. Paul told Philemon to receive Onesimus the way he would receive Paul: "So if you consider me your partner, receive him as you would receive me" (v. 17). This is perhaps as strong as anything he has said. In other words, "Philemon,

how would you see me, treat me, relate to me, receive me? Treat your former slave and new brother that way."

11. Paul said to Philemon that he would cover all Onesimus's debts: "If he has wronged you at all, or owes you anything, charge that to my account" (v. 18). Philemon would, no doubt, be shamed by this if he had any thought of demanding repayment from his new brother, because Paul was in prison! Paul lived off the gifts of others. Philemon was the one who was to prepare a guest room for Paul, not the other way around (v. 22)!

The upshot of all this is that, without *explicitly* prohibiting slavery, Paul has pointed the church away from slavery because it is an institution that is incompatible with the way the gospel works in people's lives. Whether the slavery is economic, racial, sexual, mild, or brutal, Paul's way of dealing with Philemon worked to undermine the institution across its various manifestations. To walk "in step with the truth of the gospel" (Galatians 2:14) is to walk away from slavery.

16

The Sorrows of Fathers and Sons

*Thoughts from the Lives of C. S. Lewis
and Robert Louis Stevenson*

Robert Louis Stevenson, the author of *Treasure Island,* was born in 1850 and raised in a Christian home in Scotland. His father was a civil engineer and brought up his only child to know and believe the Bible and *The Westminster Shorter Catechism.*

When Robert went to Edinburgh University, he left this childhood faith and never returned. He formed a club that had as one of its mottos, "Ignore everything that our parents taught us." His father found this written on a piece of paper and was informed by Robert that he no longer believed in the Christian faith.

The father, in an overstatement that carried the weight of sorrow, not the precision of truth, said, "You have rendered my whole life a failure."

Robert wrote to an unbelieving friend, "It was really pathetic to hear my father praying pointedly for me today at family worship, and to think the poor man's supplications were addressed to nothing better able to hear and answer than the chandelier."

The path would not be altered nor the father's sorrow—not in this life. In the end, Robert pursued a married woman, who divorced her husband to marry him. Depression was not cured by alcohol. They sailed to the Samoan Islands in the South Seas, where Robert died suddenly at age forty-four of a cerebral hemorrhage in 1894.

He wrote that "the sods cover us, and the worm that never dies, the conscience sleeps well at last, [and life is a] pilgrimage from nothing to nowhere."

A son is not a father's only life-investment, but there is none like it, and when it fails, there is no sorrow like this sorrow.*

∾

Four years after the death of Robert Louis Stevenson, another literary giant, C. S. Lewis, was born. His story of unbelief has a happier ending, but his relationship with his father was especially painful for his father, Albert.

His mother, Florence, had died of cancer when Lewis was nine. His father did not remarry. There were ample defects on both sides, father and son. But the wounding by the son was more conscious and almost brutal.

---

*My biographical sources in this meditation are Iain Murray, *The Undercover Revolution: How Fiction Changed Britain* (Edinburgh: Banner of Truth, 2009) and Alan Jacobs, *The Narnian: The Life and Imagination of C. S. Lewis* (New York: HarperCollins, 2006).

By the time Lewis was twenty, he was, to his father's dismay, an avowed atheist and probably in a sexual affair with a woman old enough to be his mother. He was also living off his father's money at Oxford University and lying to him about it all.

Albert wrote in his journal about the breakdown in his relationship with his younger son, and one explosive encounter in particular when he discovered that the young man had lied to him about his bank account:

> He said he had no respect for me—nor confidence in me.... That all my love and devotion and self-sacrifice should have come to this—that he doesn't respect me. That he doesn't trust me.... I have during the past four weeks passed through one of the most miserable periods of my life—in many respects the most miserable.... The loss of Jack's affection, if it be permanent, is irreparable and leaves me very miserable and heart sore.

Albert dared mention this pain a few months later in a letter to his son and received back a remorseless response in which the son explained how his previous bluntness was beneficial:

> As regards the other matter of which you spoke in your letters.... I am sure you will agree with me that the confidence and affection which we both desire are more likely to be restored by honest effort on both sides and toleration—such as is always necessary between imperfect human creatures—than by any answer of mine which was not perfectly sincere.

We see some truth there but no contrition.

Amazingly, both Stevenson's and Lewis's fathers kept on sending stipends to their sons through the years of rejection. In spite of words like "I am simply incapable of cohabiting any house with my father" (Stevenson) and "I really can't face him" (Lewis), the fathers kept supporting their sons.

Six years after his father's death, Lewis wrote to a friend to catch him up on the last decade: "My father is dead.... I have deep regrets about all my relations with my father (but thank God they were best at the end). I am going bald. I am a Christian."

Perhaps sending money through the broken years was the right thing to do. Perhaps not. What it shows is not approval nor that the sorrow had disappeared. Rather, it reveals a kind of bond between fathers and sons that is the foundation of pain, not its removal.

17

If You Can Be Godly and Wrong, Does Truth Matter?

*Reflections on Right Doctrine
and Right Doing*

Since there are some Arminians who are more godly than some Calvinists and some Calvinists who are more godly than some Arminians, what is the correlation between true knowledge of God and godliness? The same could be asked of different groups representing other doctrinal differences.

The best of both groups have historically admired the godliness of those in the other group. Whitefield, the Calvinist, said of Wesley, the Arminian, "Mr. Wesley, I think, is wrong in some things; yet I believe...Mr. Wesley, and others, with whom we do not agree in all things, will shine bright in glory."*

But the sad thing about our day, unlike the days of Whitefield

---

*Iain Murray, *Wesley and the Men Who Followed* (Edinburgh: Banner of Truth, 2003), 71.

and Wesley, is that many infer from this that knowing God with greater truth and fullness is not important, since it doesn't appear to be decisive in what produces godliness. But those who know what the Bible says will be protected from that mistake.

Paul correlates knowing and doing in a way that shows that knowing profoundly influences doing. Fourteen times Paul implies that our sinful behavior would be different if we knew the truth more fully. For example:

- "You yourselves wrong and defraud—even your own brothers! *Or do you not know* that the unrighteous will not inherit the kingdom of God?" (1 Corinthians 6:8–9).

- "Flee from sexual immorality…. *Or do you not know* that your body is a temple of the Holy Spirit?" (1 Corinthians 6:18–19).

- "Each one of you [should] know how to control his own body in holiness and honor, not in the passion of lust like the Gentiles *who do not know God*" (1 Thessalonians 4:4–5).

All godliness is owing to truth, that is, to God as he is truly known. Truth, known with the mind and loved with the heart, is the way God produces all godliness. "You will know the truth, and the truth will set you free" (John 8:32).

When a godlier person believes something erroneous about God, among other true things, it is not the error that God uses to produce the godliness. And when a less godly person believes something true about God, among other false things, it is not the truth that his sin uses to produce the ungodliness.

There are various reasons why a person with a more true view of

God may be less godly, and the person with a less true view of God
may be more godly:

1. The person with a less true view of God may nevertheless
   be more submissive and more powerfully influenced by the
   smaller amount of truth that he has, and the person with
   more truth may be less submissive and less influenced by
   the truth he has. The Holy Spirit (the Spirit of truth) always
   makes truth an instrument in his sanctifying influences, but
   he does not always do it in proportion to the amount of
   truth present in the mind.

   God's revealed will is that we grow in the knowledge
   of Christ (2 Peter 3:18), because in that way the Spirit can
   make our holiness the manifest fruit of what we know of
   Christ, so that Christ is more clearly honored (John 16:14).
   But the Spirit is free to make little knowledge produce much
   holiness, lest those with much knowledge be proud.

2. Two persons with radically different personalities and back-
   grounds may have more or fewer obstacles to overcome in
   the process of sanctification. Therefore, the one with fewer
   obstacles may respond in godly ways to less truth, while the
   one with more obstacles may struggle more, even though he
   has more truth.

3. A person with much truth may lag behind in godliness
   because there are hindrances that arise between the truth
   in the mind and the response of the heart to that truth.
   These hindrances may include loss of memory; ease of dis-
   traction; blind spots that keep a person from seeing how a

truth applies to a long-held pattern of behavior; mental disorders (mild or profound) that create disconnects between thoughts and volitions; confusion and ignorance about the way sanctification is meant to work; or hidden rebellion of the heart that covers itself with a veneer of orthodoxy.

Therefore, let us humble ourselves. There are clouded views that are so obscured by error that the God on the other side of the unclear glass is not the true God. So the measure of truth in our views matters infinitely. But also, there is no guarantee that right thinking will produce right living. There is more to godliness than having clear views of God. Trusting him and loving him through those views matters decisively.

18

When Does God Become 100 Percent for Us?

Were the Elect Ever Children of Wrath?

What the Bible teaches is that God becomes 100 percent irrevocably for us at the moment of justification, that is, the moment when we see Christ as a beautiful Savior and receive him as our substitute punishment and our substitute perfection. All of God's wrath, all of the condemnation we deserve, was poured out on Jesus. All of God's demands for perfect righteousness were fulfilled by Christ. The moment we see (by grace!) this Treasure and receive him in this way, his death counts as our death and his condemnation as our condemnation and his righteousness as our righteousness, and God becomes 100 percent irrevocably for us forever in that instant.

The question this leaves unanswered is, "Doesn't the Bible teach that in eternity God set his favor on us in election?" In other words, thoughtful people ask, "Did God become 100 percent for us only in the moment of faith and union with Christ and justification? Did he not become 100 percent for us in the act of election before the foundation of the world?" For example, Paul said, "[God] chose us in [Jesus] before the foundation of the world, that we should be holy and blameless before him. In love he predestined us for adoption as sons through Jesus Christ" (Ephesians 1:4–5).

Is God, then, not 100 percent for the elect from eternity? The answer hangs on the meaning of "100 percent." With the term "100 percent" I am trying to preserve a biblical truth found in several passages of Scripture. For example, in Ephesians 2:3, Paul said that Christians were "children of wrath" before they were made alive in Christ Jesus. "We all once lived [among the sons of disobedience] in the passions of our flesh, carrying out the desires of the body and the mind, and were by nature children of wrath, like the rest of mankind."

So Paul is saying that before regeneration God's wrath was on us. The elect were under wrath. This changed when God made us alive in Christ Jesus and awakened us to see the truth and beauty of Christ so that we received him as the One who died for us and as the One whose righteousness is counted as ours because of our union with Jesus. Before this happened to us, we were under God's wrath. Then, because of faith in Christ and union with him, all God's wrath was removed and he then became, in that sense, 100 percent for us.

Similarly in Romans 8:1, there is the crucial word *now*. "There is therefore *now* no condemnation for those who are in Christ Jesus." The implication of "now" is that there was once condemnation over us and now there is not. A real change in God's disposition toward us happened in the moment of our regeneration and faith and union with Christ and justification.

Notice the phrase "in Christ" at the end of this passage: "There is therefore now no condemnation for those who are *in Christ Jesus*"

(Romans 8:1). This is why God's disposition toward us is different when we believe in Christ. When we believe in Christ, we are united to him—that is, we are "in Christ." This means that his death counts as our death and his righteousness counts as our righteousness. This is why there is *now* no condemnation, whereas before there was. Before Christ bore the curse of the law and we were united to him by faith, we were under the curse of the law. "Christ redeemed us from the curse of the law by becoming a curse for us" (Galatians 3:13).

When Paul used the language of God being "for us," it was in the context of what Christ has done for us in history. For example, Romans 8:31–32 says, "If God is for us, who can be against us? He who did not spare his own Son but gave him up for us all, how will he not also with him graciously give us all things?" Not sparing his Son is the act that secures God's being 100 percent for us forever.

So was God 100 percent for us from eternity because we were elect? Consider this analogy. Before justification, the elect were under the "sentence" of God's wrath but not the actual experience of its outpouring. For the elect to be born "children of wrath" (Ephesians 2:3) and to be "condemned already" (John 3:18) prior to conversion does not mean that the elect were enduring the *actual* wrath of God that is equivalent to what the nonelect experience in hell. It means that the *sentence* of God's wrath still hung over them.

So there is a real sense we can indeed say that God was 100 percent for the elect before we were justified. He was 100 percent certain that the sentence that hung over us would not be executed. He was 100 percent certain that he would bring us to faith and save us.

But when I ask, when did God become 100 percent for us? I mean more than, when did it become 100 percent certain that God would save us?" I mean, when did it happen that God was for us and *only* for us? That is, when did it happen that the only disposition of God toward us was mercy? Or, when did God become for us so fully that there was not any wrath or curse or condemnation on us, but only mercy?

The answer, I still say, is at the point when, by grace, we saw Christ as a supremely valuable Savior and received him as our substitute sacrifice and substitute righteousness. In other words, it happened at the point of justification. The implication of this is that all our works, all our perseverance, all our continuing faith and obedience does not cause God to be 100 percent for us, but is the *result* of his being 100 percent for us. This is a hugely important distinction for your own soul, and how you press on in the fight of faith. As Paul said, "I press on to make it my own, *because* Christ Jesus has made me his own" (Philippians 3:12)—100 percent his own.

Paul's logic in Romans 8:32 is that because God gave his Son to die for us, therefore he will give us all things with him. That is, God will see to it that we persevere to the end, not only because we are elect, but because Christ died for us and we are in Christ. That is the logic of 1 Corinthians 1:8–9: "[God] will sustain you to the end, guiltless in the day of our Lord Jesus Christ. God is faithful, *by whom you were called* into the fellowship of his Son, Jesus Christ our Lord." The call is mentioned as the ground of God's faithfulness to sustain us to the end.

Therefore, exult in the truth that God will keep you. He will get you to the end because in Christ he is 100 percent for you. And therefore, getting to the end does not make God to be 100 percent for you. It is the effect of the fact that he is already totally for you.

19

Feeding My Soul in
Four Parts of the Bible

A Glimpse of My Morning
Strolls in God's Garden

I hope you are reading your Bible steadily throughout the year. I hope you don't miss a day. The blessed person whose life is like a tree planted by streams of water savors the Word of God every day. "On his law he meditates day and night" (Psalm 1:2). I pray that there are times when it tastes so good, you slow down and steep your heart in it. Here is what often happens when you set your face like flint to see and savor God in his Word every day.

I was reading in four parts of the Bible, not for any ministry preparation, but just to feed my soul. In every text, another text came to mind that made each clearer. And that blew some fog away so I could see and enjoy God more fully. So this meditation is not unified by a theme. It's a glimpse of what happens often in my morning stroll through the beautiful and nourishing garden of God's Word. Come with me to four very different parts of the garden.

1. Why did Saul die?

- "Saul took his own sword and fell upon it" (1 Chronicles 10:4).
- "So Saul died for his breach of faith. He broke faith with the LORD in that he did not keep the command of the LORD, and also consulted a medium" (1 Chronicles 10:13).
- "The LORD put him to death" (1 Chronicles 10:14).

One reason Saul died is that he committed suicide. Another is that he broke faith with the Lord much earlier. Another is that God put him to death. None of these excludes the others. To say God is the decisive actor does not mean Saul did not act. To say there are physical causes for a death (suicide) does not mean there were not moral causes (unfaithfulness).

To say that Saul brought his demise on himself (by unfaithfulness and suicide) does not mean God did not bring it on him. We would be unfaithful to Scripture if all we said was that the reason Saul died was the natural consequence of his own behavior. We must also say, "The LORD put him to death."

There was real punishment, not just impersonal, natural consequences. God is personal. God put him to death. There was punishment by a judge and executioner. There was wrath. The Bible is designed to make sure we do not turn death and hell into impersonal consequences. "The LORD put him to death."

Therefore, I was sobered as I read. I trembled in my spirit. I bowed to God's right and authority to give and take life. I reverenced him. Blessed be the name of the Lord.

2. Who will benefit from promises made to David?

- "I will make a horn to sprout for David; I have prepared a lamp for my anointed. His enemies I will
  clothe with shame, but on him his crown will shine"
  (Psalm 132:17–18).

- "Come, everyone who thirsts, come to the waters; and he
  who has no money, come, buy and eat!… And I will
  make with you an everlasting covenant, my steadfast,
  sure love for David" (Isaiah 55:1, 3).

Whoever comes to God through Jesus Christ, his Son, thirsting
for what he is, rather than depending on who we are or what we do,
God will make with that one a covenant.

What covenant? A covenant defined and secured by God's "sure
love for David." I take that to mean that I am included in the Davidic
covenant. What David gets I will get in Christ Jesus.

And what does that include? A horn will sprout for me. That is,
great strength will fight for me and protect me. There will be a God-
prepared lamp for me. So light will surround me and darkness will
not overcome me. There will be a crown for me—I will reign with the
Son of David and sit with him on his throne. "The one who conquers,
I will grant him to sit with me on my throne" (Revelation 3:21).

It is an astonishing thing that I will benefit from the promises
made to David. God means for me to be astonished. He means for me
to leave my devotions astonished at the power and authority and
surety with which I am loved by God.

3. Do everything in the name of Jesus.

- "Whatever you do, in word or deed, do everything in the
  name of the Lord Jesus" (Colossians 3:17).

- "The seventy-two returned with joy, saying, 'Lord, even the demons are subject to us in your name!'" (Luke 10:17).

Do everything with a sense of dependence on the power and authority of the Lord Jesus. Do everything with a view to Jesus being honored in it. Do everything with a view to others being helped by Jesus in it. These two passages speak of the pervasiveness (everything, Colossians 3:17) and the power (subjected demons, Luke 10:17) of the name of Jesus in the life of an obedient Christian. Let it be that pervasive, and let it bring that much power.

4. Who forgives whom first?

- "Forgive us our sins, for we ourselves forgive everyone who is indebted to us" (Luke 11:4).
- "As the Lord has forgiven you, so you also must forgive" (Colossians 3:13).

When Jesus teaches us to pray that God forgive us "for we ourselves forgive," he is not saying that the first move in forgiveness is our move. Rather it goes like this: God forgave us when we believed in Christ (Acts 10:43). Then, from this broken, joyful, grateful, hopeful, experience of being forgiven, we offer forgiveness to others. This signifies that we have been "savingly" forgiven. That is, our forgiving others shows that we have faith; we are united to Christ; we are indwelt by the Spirit.

But we still sin (1 John 1:8, 10). So we still turn to God for fresh applications of the work of Christ on our behalf, fresh applications of forgiveness. We cannot do this with any confidence if we are harboring an unforgiving spirit (Matthew, 18:23–35). That's why Jesus says we ask for forgiveness because we are forgiving. This is like saying:

"Father, continue to extend to me the mercies purchased by Christ because by these mercies I forsake vengeance and extend to others what you have extended to me."

O, how sweet is the Word of God! I looked out my window into the bright morning and said, *"I love you, God. I love you, Lord Jesus. I love your Word. O, what a privilege to know you and to have your Word. Please keep me faithful to it. In Jesus' name. Amen."*

20

Gleaning Truth from G. K. Chesterton

How a Roman Catholic Can Serve Today's Happy Calvinists

G. K. Chesterton was a British journalist and a brilliant writer. Nobody exploits the power of paradox like Chesterton. I heartily recommend his book *Orthodoxy*.

The title gives scarcely a clue as to what you will find inside. It had a huge influence on me forty years ago in ways that would have exasperated Chesterton. He did all he could to keep me from becoming a Calvinist, and instead made me a romantic one—a happy one.

If I thought his broadsides against predestination really hit home and undid true biblical doctrine, I would keep my mouth shut or change my worldview. But his celebration of poetry and paradox undermines his own abomination of the greatest truth-and-mystery-lovers around today, the happy Calvinists.

Nothing in this Calvinism-abominating book came close to keeping me from embracing the glorious sovereignty of God. On the contrary, the poetic brightness of the book, along with the works of C. S. Lewis, awakened in me an exuberance about the strangeness of all things, which in the end made me able to embrace the imponderable paradoxes of God's decisive control of all things and the total justice of his holding us accountable.

One of the reasons that Calvinism is stirring today is that it takes both truth and mystery seriously. It's a singing, poetry-writing, running-through-the-fields Calvinism.

It's the Arminians who are the rationalists. Arminianism trumps biblical sentences with metaphysics: God can't control all things and hold us responsible. God can't choose some and love all. Why? Metaphysics. Out with mystery! It just can't be!

So Chesterton's anti-Calvinist shotgun sprays all around today's poet-Calvinist and misses the mark.

Read *Orthodoxy.*

A few of you may be swept away into the folly of Roman Catholic sacramentalism. A few others may be confirmed in your tiff with joyless Calvinists. But for many readers, especially the Bible-saturated ones, this book will awaken such a sense of wonder in you that you will not feel at home again until you enter the new world of the wide-eyed children called the happy Reformed.

Here is a flavor of what to expect in *Orthodoxy:**

- "[This book] recounts my elephantine adventures in pursuit of the obvious." (12)
- "It is one thing to describe an interview with a...creature that does not exist. It is another thing to discover that

---

*Page numbers are from my 1959 edition by Doubleday and Co., Garden City, New York.

the rhinoceros does exist and then take pleasure in the fact that he looks as if he didn't." (11)

- "Exactly what does breed insanity is reason. Poets do not go mad; but chess-players do. Mathematicians go mad, and cashiers; but creative artists very seldom." (17)
- "Only one great English poet went mad, Cowper. And he was definitely driven mad by logic, by the ugly and alien logic of predestination. Poetry was not the disease but the medicine.... He was damned by John Calvin." (17)
- "The poet only desires exaltation and expansion, a world to stretch himself in. The poet only asks to get his head into the heavens. It is the logician who seeks to get the heavens into his head. And it is his head that splits." (17)
- "The madman is not the man who has lost his reason. The madman is the man who has lost everything but his reason." (19)
- "Mysticism keeps men sane. As long as you have mystery you have health. When you destroy mystery you create morbidity." (28)
- "The ordinary man...has always cared more for truth than for consistency. If he saw two truths that seemed to contradict each other, he would take the two truths and the contradictions along with them." (28)
- "When we are very young children we do not need fairy tales: we only need tales. Mere life is interesting enough. A child of seven is excited by being told that Tommy opened the door and saw a dragon. But a child of three is excited by being told that Tommy opened a door." (54)

- "Man is more himself, man is more manlike, when joy is the fundamental thing in him, and grief the superficial. Melancholy should be an innocent interlude, a tender and fugitive frame of mind; praise should be the permanent pulsation of the soul. Pessimism is at best an emotional half-holiday; joy is the uproarious labor by which all things live." (159)

- "Tradition means giving votes to the most obscure of all classes, our ancestors. It is the democracy of the dead. Tradition refuses to submit to the small and arrogant oligarchy of those who merely happen to be walking about." (48)

How can I not give thanks for this jolly Catholic whose only cranky side seemed to be his clouded views of happy Calvinists!

21

What's the Place of Confrontation in Marriage?

Guidance from Ephesians 5:25–27

Sometimes I finish sermons in articles and books. This is one of those finishings. I preached a sermon originally titled "Marriage: Confronting, Forgiving, Forbearing." In the end, I struck the word *confronting*—not because it shouldn't happen, but because I had no time. So this is what I would have said if there had been time.

Focusing on forgiving and forbearing might give the impression that none of our sinful traits or annoying idiosyncrasies ever changes. All you do is forgive and forbear. But that's not true. God gives grace, not only to forgive and to forbear, but also to change so that less forgiving and forbearing are needed. That too is a gift of grace. Grace is not just power to return good for evil but also power to do less evil— even power to be less bothersome.

But I have approached this by putting the emphasis on forgiveness and forbearance first, not on change. The reason is because gracious forgiveness and forbearance are the rock-solid foundation on which the call for change can be heard with hope and security rather than fear and a sense of being threatened. Only when a wife or husband feels that the other is totally committed—even if he or she doesn't change—can the call for change feel like grace rather than an ultimatum.

So a message on forgiveness and forbearance came first. But now I am emphasizing that marriage should not be—and, God willing, need not be—a static stretch of time inhabited by changeless personalities in persistent conflict. Even that is better than divorce in God's eyes and has a glory of its own. But it is not the best picture of Christ and the church. The durability of the relationship, in spite of conflict, tells the truth about Christ and the church. The unwillingness to change does not.

In Christ's relationship to the church, he is clearly seeking the transformation of his bride into something morally and spiritually beautiful. This is plain in Ephesians 5:25–27.

> Husbands, love your wives, as Christ loved the church and gave himself up for her, that he might sanctify her, having cleansed her by the washing of water with the word, so that he might present the church to himself in splendor, without spot or wrinkle or any such thing, that she might be holy and without blemish.

This implies that the husband, who is to love like Christ, bears a unique responsibility for the moral and spiritual growth of his wife, which means that over time she will change.

If a husband is loving and wise, this will feel, to a humble wife, like she is being served, not humiliated. Christ died to purify his bride. Moreover, Christ not only died to sanctify his bride, he goes on speaking to her in his Word with a view to applying his sacrifice to her for her transformation. Similarly, the wise and loving husband seeks to speak in a way that brings his wife more and more into conformity to Christ.

Submission does not mean that a wife cannot seek the transformation of her husband, even while respecting him as her head: her leader, protector, and provider. There are several reasons I say this. One is that prayer is something that the church does toward God through Christ with a view to asking him to do things a certain way. If we are sick, we ask him for healing. If we are hungry, we ask for our daily bread. If we are lost, we ask for direction. And so on. Since we believe in the absolute sovereignty of Christ to govern all things, this means that we look at the present situation that he has ordained, and we ask him to change it. That's what prayer is. And it's not inconsistent with Christ's sovereignty.

Prayer is only an analogy to what the wife does toward her husband. We never "confront" Jesus with his imperfection and seek his change. He has no imperfections. But we do seek from him changes in the situation he has brought about, because it may well be his will to change them. That is what petitionary prayer is. So wives, in this analogy, will ask their husbands that some things be changed in the way he is doing things.

But the main reason we can say that wives should seek their husbands' transformation is that husbands are only similar to Christ in the relationship with their wives. They are not Christ. And one of the main differences is that husbands need to change and Christ doesn't. When Paul said, "The husband is the head of the wife even *as* Christ is the head of the church" (Ephesians 5:23), the word *as* does not mean that husbands are identical to Christ in authority or perfection or wisdom or grace or in any other way. They are not "equal to" Christ; they are "as" Christ. They are, unlike Christ, sinful and finite and fallible. They need to change.

Wives are not only submissive wives; they are also loving sisters. There is a unique way for a submissive wife to be a caring sister toward her imperfect brother-husband. She will, from time to time, follow Galatians 6:1 in his case: "If anyone is caught in any transgression, you who are spiritual should restore him in a spirit of gentleness." She will do that for him.

Both of them will obey Matthew 18:15 as necessary and will do so in the unique demeanor and context called for by headship and submission: "If your brother sins against you, go and tell him his fault, between you and him alone."

So from these and other observations that could be made from the New Testament, I hope it is clear that a faithful, covenant-keeping marriage is not merely forgiving and forbearing. It is also confronting—in loving and wise ways formed by the calling of headship and submission. To see how I worked all this out more fully, the sermon series actually made its way into a book called *This Momentary Marriage: A Parable of Permanence.*

22

Changed Lives in Jesus' New Life

Radical Effects of the Resurrection

If in Christ we have hope in this life only, we are of all people most to be pitied.... Why are we in danger every hour?

—1 CORINTHIANS 15:19, 30

I protest, brothers, by my pride in you, which I have in Christ Jesus our Lord, I die every day! What do I gain if, humanly speaking, I fought with beasts at Ephesus? If the dead are not raised, "Let us eat and drink, for tomorrow we die."

—1 CORINTHIANS 15:31–32

But in fact Christ has been raised from the dead, the firstfruits of those who have fallen asleep.

—1 CORINTHIANS 15:20

P aul pondered how he would assess his lifestyle if there were no resurrection from the dead. He said it would be ridiculous— pitiable (1 Corinthians 15:19). The resurrection guided and empowered him to do things that would be ludicrous without the hope of resurrection.

For example, Paul looked at all the dangers he willingly faced. He said they come "every hour" (v. 30).

> On frequent journeys, in *danger* from rivers, *danger* from robbers, *danger* from my own people, *danger* from Gentiles, *danger* in the city, *danger* in the wilderness, *danger* at sea, *danger* from false brothers. (2 Corinthians 11:26)

Then he considered the extent of his self-denial and said, "I die every day!" (1 Corinthians 15:31). This is Paul's experience of what Jesus said in Luke 9:23, "If anyone would come after me, let him deny himself and take up his cross daily and follow me." I take this to mean that there was something pleasant that Paul had to put to death every day. No day was without the death of some desire.

> With far greater labors, far more imprisonments, with countless beatings, and often near death. Five times I received at the hands of the Jews the forty lashes less one. Three times I was beaten with rods. Once I was stoned. Three times I was shipwrecked; a night and a day I was adrift at sea;… in toil and hardship, through many a sleepless night, in hunger and thirst, often without food, in cold and exposure. And, apart from other things, there is the daily pressure on me of my anxiety for all the churches. (2 Corinthians 11:23–28)

Then he recalled that he "fought with beasts at Ephesus" (1 Corinthians 15:32). We don't know what he is referring to. A certain kind of opponent to the gospel is called a beast in 2 Peter 2:12 and Jude 10. In any case, it was utterly disheartening. "We do not want you to be unaware, brothers, of the affliction we experienced in Asia. For we were so utterly burdened beyond our strength that we despaired of life itself" (2 Corinthians 1:8).

So Paul concluded from his hourly danger and his daily dying and his fighting with beasts that the life he had chosen in following Jesus was foolish and pitiable if he would not be raised from the dead: "If in Christ we have hope in this life only, we are of all people most to be pitied" (1 Corinthians 15:19). In other words, only the resurrection with Christ and the joys of eternity can make sense out of this voluntary suffering.

If death were the end of the matter, he said, "Let us eat and drink, for tomorrow we die" (1 Corinthians 15:32). This doesn't mean let's all become gluttons and drunkards. They are pitiable too, with or without the resurrection. He means if there is no resurrection, what makes sense is middle-class moderation to maximize earthly pleasures.

But that is not what Paul chose. He chose suffering, because he chose obedience. When Ananias came to him at his conversion with the words from the Lord Jesus, "I will show him how much he must suffer for the sake of my name" (Acts 9:16), Paul accepted this as part of his calling. Suffer he must.

How could Paul do it? What was the source of this radical obedience? The answer is this: "In fact Christ has been raised from the dead, the firstfruits of those who have fallen asleep" (1 Corinthians 15:20). In other words, Christ was raised, and Paul will be raised with him. Therefore, nothing suffered for Jesus is in vain (1 Corinthians 15:58).

The hope of the resurrection radically changed the way Paul lived. It freed him from materialism and consumerism. It gave him the power to go without things that many people feel they must have in this life. For example, though he had the right to marry (1 Corinthians 9:5), he renounced that pleasure because he was called to bear so much suffering. This he did because of the resurrection.

This is the way Jesus said the hope of the resurrection is supposed to change our behavior. For example, he told us to invite to our homes people who cannot pay us back in this life. How are we to be motivated to do this? Jesus said, "You will be repaid at the resurrection of the just" (Luke 14:14).

This is a radical call for us to look hard at our present lives to see if they are shaped by the hope of the resurrection. Do we make decisions on the basis of gain in this world or gain in the next? Do we take risks for love's sake that can only be explained as wise if there is a resurrection?

Do we lose heart when our bodies give way to the aging process and we have to admit that we will never do certain things again? Or do we look to the resurrection and take heart?

> We do not lose heart. Though our outer self is wasting away, our inner self is being renewed day by day. For this light momentary affliction is preparing for us an eternal weight of glory beyond all comparison. (2 Corinthians 4:16–17)

May God give us the grace to rededicate ourselves to a lifetime of letting the resurrection have its radical effects.

23

How God Teaches the Deep Things of His Word

A Meditation on Psalm 119:65–72

You have dealt well with your servant,
 O LORD, according to your word.
Teach me good judgment and knowledge,
 for I believe in your commandments.
Before I was afflicted I went astray,
 but now I keep your word.
You are good and do good;
 teach me your statutes.
The insolent smear me with lies,
 but with my whole heart I keep your precepts;
their heart is unfeeling like fat,
 but I delight in your law.
It is good for me that I was afflicted,
 that I might learn your statutes.
The law of your mouth is better to me
 than thousands of gold and silver pieces.

—PSALM 119:65–72

The reason Psalm 119 has 176 verses is that the Hebrew alphabet has twenty-two letters. The psalmist exults in the multifaceted preciousness of God's Word by taking each letter of the alphabet and writing eight verses of exultation, each verse beginning with that letter. It's like saying: "The Word of God is precious in every way from A to Z—beyond perfection." Eight is one more than seven, the number of completeness and perfection.

Ordinarily in each group of eight verses, the psalmist uses mostly different words that start with the letter for that section of the acrostic. For example, the verses beginning with the letter *heth* (vv. 57–64) use eight different words beginning with that letter. But verses 65–72, which start with the Hebrew letter *teth,* stand out, because they begin with the same word five times—the word *good (tov)*. This makes us sit up and take notice.

Something really good is being emphasized. What is the good he wants us to see?

Here is my translation in awkward English that lets you see the prominence of the word *good*.

65: Good *(tov)* you did, Yahweh, with your servant according to your word.

66: Good *(tov)* discernment and knowledge teach me, because in your commandments I trust.

67: Before I was afflicted I erred, but now I keep your word.

68: Good *(tov)* you are, and you cause good to happen. Teach me your statutes.

69: Smear upon me lies—so do the proud—but I, with all my heart, watch your precepts.

70: Gross like fat is their heart. I delight in your instruction.

71: Good for me *(tov li)*. I was afflicted so that I might learn your statutes.

72: Good for me *(tov li)* is the instruction of your mouth, more than thousands of gold and silver pieces.

These are not random comments about what is good. They are connected, and a specific good is in mind.

Verse 65 says that God did something good: Good you did, Yahweh, with your servant according to your word. The good he did accords with his word. That means God's Word is designed for our good and that what God does to help us go deep with his Word is good. What did he do that makes the psalmist write this?

In verse 66 the psalmist prays that God would give him good discernment *because he trusts in God's commandments.* That means God does not bless with discernment a negative attitude toward his word. If we trust that his words are the best counsel in the world, he will give us discernment when we ask.

So the psalmist pleads for a mind and heart that penetrates deep into the Word of God and becomes spiritually discerning for all the hundreds of situations that are not addressed directly by the Bible. So he prays—and we should pray—*God, do whatever you must do to teach me your Word.*

Verse 67 tells us what God did to answer this prayer for biblical discernment: "Before I was afflicted I went astray, but now I keep your word." God sent affliction. And this affliction was a profound teacher. It moved the psalmist into deeper obedience: Now—after the affliction—"I keep your word." We see not only obedience but also understanding.

Verse 71: Good it was for me that I was afflicted, so that I might learn your statutes. Affliction brought learning. This is the discernment he had prayed for.

So the good that God did (v. 65) was Bible-illumining, discernment-giving, obedience-producing affliction. What was the affliction? It was slander from spiritually hardened adversaries.

Verse 69: The proud smear me with lies, but I with all my heart watch your precepts.

This is the good the psalmist wants us to see.

Verse 68: Good you are, and you cause good to happen. The good is the affliction that brings about understanding, discernment, and obedience. Good it was for me that I was afflicted, so that I might learn your statutes (v. 71).

How can he call affliction *good*? It's because in his value-scheme, penetrating insight into God's Word is more valuable than thousands of gold and silver pieces—or freedom from affliction.

Verse 72: Good to me is the instruction of your mouth, more than thousands of gold and silver pieces. If God and his word are your highest values—your greatest desires—then whatever helps you know them and experience them deeply will be good—not easy, and maybe not even morally right (like slander from your adversaries), but good in the sense that God ordains it to give you what is absolutely best—the illumining effect of God's infinitely valuable word.

In Martin Luther's meditation on these verses he said that trials *(Anfechtungen)* were one of his best teachers:

> I want you to know how to study theology in the right way. I
> have practiced this method myself.... Here you will find three
> rules. They are frequently proposed throughout Psalm [119]

and run thus: *Oratio, meditatio, tentatio* (Prayer, meditation, trial).… [Trials] teach you not only to know and understand but also to experience how right, how true, how sweet, how lovely, how mighty, how comforting God's word is: it is wisdom supreme.

As soon as God's word becomes known through you, the devil will afflict you…and will teach you by his temptations to seek and to love God's word. For I myself…owe my papists many thanks for so beating, pressing, and frightening me through the devil's raging that they have turned me into a fairly good theologian, driving me to a goal I should never have reached.*

Lord, incline our hearts to your Word and not to gold and silver. Make us cherish your Word so much that we embrace whatever it takes to give us understanding and good discernment and faithful obedience.

And when it comes, give us the grace to say, "Good you are, and you cause good to happen."

---

*Martin Luther, *What Luther Says: An Anthology,* compiler Ewald M. Plass (St. Louis: Concordia, 1986), 1359–60.

24

How Shall We Love Our Muslim Neighbor?

Winning Them to Jesus by Echoing His Love

There are as many answers to the question, How shall we love our Muslim neighbor? as there are ways to do good and not wrong. "Love does no wrong to a neighbor" (Romans 13:10). "Love bears all things, believes all things, hopes all things, endures all things" (1 Corinthians 13:7). Below I give nine ways of loving Muslims that I think need to be emphasized in our day.

No human beings are excluded from the love of Christians—not the closest friend, and not the worst enemy. "Love your enemies and pray for those who persecute you" (Matthew 5:44). The mention of loving our enemies is not meant to imply that all Muslims feel or act with enmity toward Christians. They don't. They are often hospitable and kind and caring. The point is, even when someone treats us with enmity (of whatever religion or nonreligion), we should continue loving. So when I refer to loving our enemies in the points below, keep in mind that I do so not to imply all Muslims are our enemies but to make sure that none is excluded.

Another clarification is needed in our contemporary context. When I say in what follows that love calls us to do good in practical ways that meet physical needs, I do not mean that this help is offered contingent on Muslims becoming Christians. To be sure, every act of love, no matter how practical, longs for the eternal good of the one being loved. We always aim for the salvation of the people we love, no matter what we are doing for them. But we don't stop loving if they are unresponsive. Practical love is a witness to the love of Christ. Witness is not withheld where it is needed most. Conversions coerced by force or finances contradict the very nature of saving faith. Saving faith is a free embrace of Jesus as our Savior, Lord, and highest Treasure. He is not a mere means to treasure. He is the Treasure.

Here is how we can extend ourselves in love toward Muslim people.

1. Pray the fullest blessing of Christ on them whether they love you or not.

- "Bless those who curse you, pray for those who abuse you" (Luke 6:28).
- "Bless those who persecute you; bless and do not curse them" (Romans 12:14).
- "When reviled, we bless" (1 Corinthians 4:12).

2. Do good to them in practical ways that meet their physical needs.

- "Love your enemies, do good to those who hate you" (Luke 6:27).

- "As you wish that others would do to you, do so to them" (Luke 6:31).
- "See that no one repays anyone evil for evil, but always seek to do good to one another and to everyone" (1 Thessalonians 5:15).
- "If your enemy is hungry, feed him; if he is thirsty, give him something to drink; for by so doing you will heap burning coals on his head" (Romans 12:20).

3. Do not retaliate when you're personally wronged.

- "Do not repay evil for evil or reviling for reviling, but on the contrary, bless, for to this you were called, that you may obtain a blessing" (1 Peter 3:9).
- "Repay no one evil for evil.... Beloved, never avenge yourselves, but leave it to the wrath of God, for it is written, 'Vengeance is mine, I will repay, says the Lord'" (Romans 12:17, 19).

4. Live peaceably with them as much as it depends on you.

- "If possible, so far as it depends on you, live peaceably with all" (Romans 12:18).

5. Pursue their joyful freedom from sin and from condemnation by telling them the truth of Christ.

- "Jesus said to the Jews who had believed him, 'If you abide in my word, you are truly my disciples, and you will know the truth, and the truth will set you free'" (John 8:31–32).

6. Earnestly desire that they join you in heaven with the Father by showing them the way, Jesus Christ.

- "Brothers, my heart's desire...for them is that they may be saved" (Romans 10:1).
- "Jesus said to him, 'I am the way, and the truth, and the life. No one comes to the Father except through me'" (John 14:6).
- "Whoever believes in him should not perish but have eternal life" (John 3:16).

7. Seek to comprehend the meaning of what they say, so that your affirmations or criticisms are based on true understanding, not distortion or caricature.

- "[Love] does not rejoice at wrongdoing, but rejoices with the truth" (1 Corinthians 13:6).

8. Warn them with tears that those who do not receive Jesus Christ as the crucified and risen Savior, who takes away the sins of the world, will perish under the wrath of God.

- "To all who did receive him, who believed in his name, he gave the right to become children of God" (John 1:12).
- "If you confess with your mouth that Jesus is Lord and believe in your heart that God raised him from the dead, you will be saved" (Romans 10:9).
- "For many, of whom I have often told you and now tell you even with tears, walk as enemies of the cross of Christ" (Philippians 3:18).

9. Don't mislead them or give them false hope by saying, "Muslims worship the true God."

This statement communicates to almost everybody a positive picture of the Muslim heart knowing, loving, and honoring the true God. But Jesus makes a person's response to himself the litmus test of the authenticity of a person's response to God. And he is explicit that if a person rejects him as the Divine One who gave his life as a ransom for sins and rose again—that person does not know, love, or honor the true God.

- "They said to [Jesus] therefore, 'Where is your Father?' Jesus answered, 'You know neither me nor my Father. If you knew me, you would know my Father also'" (John 8:19).
- "Whoever does not honor the Son does not honor the Father who sent him" (John 5:23).
- "[Jesus said,] 'I know that you do not have the love of God within you. I have come in my Father's name, and you do not receive me'" (John 5:42–43).

We do not mislead Muslims, or those who care about Muslims, by saying that they "know" or "honor" and "love" the true God when they do not receive Jesus for who he really is. We cannot see people's hearts. How do we know if they know and honor and love the true God? We lay down our lives to offer them Jesus. If they receive him, they know and love and honor God. If they don't, they don't. Jesus is the test.

That was Jesus' point when he said, "The one who rejects me rejects him who sent me" (Luke 10:16). And, "Whoever receives me receives him who sent me" (Matthew 10:40). And, "If you believed Moses, you would believe me" (John 5:46).

The most loving thing we can do for Muslims, or anyone else, is to tell them the whole truth about Jesus Christ, in the context of sacrificial care for them and willingness to suffer for them rather than abandon them. And then plead with them to turn away from vain worship (Mark 7:7) and receive Christ as the crucified and risen Savior for the forgiveness of their sins and the hope of eternal life. Our great joy would be to have brothers and sisters from all the Muslim peoples of the world.

25

What Love Does
and Does Not Do

*An Anniversary Meditation
on 1 Corinthians 13:4–7*

Love is patient and kind; love does not envy or boast;
it is not arrogant or rude. It does not insist on its
own way; it is not irritable or resentful; it does not
rejoice at wrongdoing, but rejoices with the truth.
Love bears all things, believes all things, hopes all
things, endures all things.

—1 CORINTHIANS 13:4–7

Noël and I pondered and prayed over 1 Corinthians 13 on our
recent wedding anniversary. As a tradition we pick a portion of
Scripture and pray our way through it on our anniversary. We turn it
into thanks and praises and requests for ourselves and our family and
the church and the world. Mainly, we focus on our own shortcomings

with a view to improvement. We seek God's grace and power to turn biblical truth into real life. So this time we focused on 1 Corinthians 13, especially verses 4–7.

What is Paul doing here? He says fifteen things about what love does and does not do. When you ponder the list, it is peculiar. If you come expecting a definition of love, it doesn't work very well. Crucial things seem to be missing. Think about other places where the core of love is defined: John 15:13, "Greater love has no one than this, that someone lay down his life for his friends." First John 4:10, "In this is love…that he loved us and sent his Son to be the propitiation for our sins." Romans 5:8, "God shows his love for us in that while we were still sinners, Christ died for us." At the core of love is a self-sacrificing pursuit of the beloved's greatest good. Love saves. Love rescues. Love helps. And it does so, if necessary, at cost to the lover.

But this core element of helping another person is not the stress in 1 Corinthians 13:4–7. When you try to group the fifteen elements into categories, there are two big ones: (1) statements about how love is durable and doesn't give up, and (2) statements about how love is not proud. Thirteen of the fifteen elements seem to fit into these two categories. Of the remaining two elements, one comes close to the proactive helpfulness (as opposed to reactive patience), namely, "love is kind." The other stresses that love rejoices when truth holds sway. So here is one way to categorize what love is and is not:

Enduring (Not Fragile)

- is patient (long-suffering)
- bears all things
- believes all things

- hopes all things
- endures all things

Humble (Not Proud)

- isn't envious or jealous
- isn't boastful or proud
- isn't arrogant or puffed up
- isn't rude or offensive
- doesn't insist on own way or seek its own
- isn't irritable or easily peeved
- isn't resentful or keep an account of wrongs
- doesn't rejoice at wrongdoing or boast of licentious freedom

Pro-kindness and Truth

- is kind
- rejoices with the truth and glad for the truth to advance

What I conclude from this is that Paul was not trying to define *love* in the abstract. He was laying love as a grid over the messed up Corinthian church, where he saw all these pride-based negative behaviors and said their attitudes and behaviors were *not* how love acts or feels. They were boasting in men (3:21). They were puffed up, even in wrongdoing (5:1–2). They were unwilling to suffer long and bear all things and so were taking each other to court (6:1–8). They were insisting on their own way in eating meat that caused others to stumble (8:11–12). They were acting in rude or unseemly ways, not wearing the customary head coverings (11:1–16). They were insisting on their own way as they ate their own meal at the Lord's Supper without any regard to others (11:21–22). They were jealous and envious as they compared their spiritual gifts and thought that some were needed and others were not (12:21–22).

In other words, Paul is not defining love. He is applying love to the Corinthians' situation and using it as the criterion for why some of their attitudes and behaviors are unacceptable.

But this is not less useful for us. Noël and I saw immediately how relevant these categories were for us. The first category (endurance) says that wherever there is love there is pain—love *suffers* long *(makrothumia), endures* all things, *bears* all things. This is realism and therefore comforting. If two people, or two thousand people, are in a relationship of love, all will be hurt sooner or later. And all will need to "suffer long" and endure and bear. It struck us as amazing that this was so prominent in Paul's treatment of love. So we prayed hard that we would be good lovers in this way (giving less offense and taking less offense).

Then even more penetrating is the major emphasis on pride. Is it not surprising that the opposite of love in 1 Corinthians 13 is not hate but pride? The main category of what love does not do is "arrogance" (boasting, seeking its own way). So we set ourselves to self-examination and prayer again: *O Lord, reveal and destroy the pride in our lives.*

And of course, even though they are in a small category, the other two elements of love are huge: Be kind. And be happy about the prevailing of truth. So that too is our prayer for our marriage.

I offer Noël and me simply as an example. This is all for your sake. Married or single, you can apply the patterns of love in 1 Corinthians

13 to your situation. May I even be so bold as to ask that you pray for us. As I write this, we have been married for almost forty-five years.

Verses 4–7 of this beautiful love chapter would be a great prayer list for any couple. I am praying for you as I close this chapter. O that we all might never stop growing "in the grace [love!] and knowledge of our Lord and Savior Jesus Christ" (2 Peter 3:18).

26

Putting My Daughter to Bed After the Bridge Collapsed

What Do Tragedies Like This Mean for Us?

At about 6 p.m. on August 1, 2007, the I-35W highway bridge over the Mississippi River in Minneapolis collapsed. The bridge was located within sight of our church. Most of us who ministered at the church crossed this bridge several times a week. Some who were heading home that day had been on the bridge fifteen minutes before it collapsed. Thirteen people died in the collapse. Writing from this distance today, that seems miraculous. It was rush hour and the bridge was full of cars. But that first night we knew little and expected much loss of life.

For our family devotions that evening our appointed reading was Luke 13:1–9. It was not my choice. This is surely no coincidence. I thought, *O that all of the Twin Cities, in shock at this major calamity, would hear what Jesus has to say about it from Luke's passage.* People came to Jesus with heart-wrenching news about the slaughter of worshipers by Pilate. Here is what he said:

> There were some present at that very time who told him about the Galileans whose blood Pilate had mingled with their sacrifices. And he answered them, "Do you think that these Galileans were worse sinners than all the other Galileans, because they suffered in this way? No, I tell you; but unless you repent, you will all likewise perish. Or those eighteen on whom the tower in Siloam fell and killed them: do you think that they were worse offenders than all the others who lived in Jerusalem? No, I tell you; but unless you repent, you will all likewise perish." (Luke 13:1–5)

Jesus implied that those who brought him this news thought he would say that those who died deserved to die and that those who didn't die did not deserve to die. That is not what he said. He said everyone deserves to die. And if you and I don't repent, we too will perish. This is a stunning response. It only makes sense from a view of reality that is radically oriented on God.

All of us have sinned against God, not just against man. This is an outrage ten thousand times worse than the collapse of the I-35W bridge. That any human is breathing at this minute on this planet is sheer mercy from God. God makes the sun rise and the rain fall on those who do not treasure him above all else. He causes the heart to beat and the lungs to work for millions of people who deserve his wrath. This is a view of reality that desperately needs to be taught in our churches so that we are prepared for the calamities of the world.

The meaning of that bridge's collapse was that John Piper is a sinner and should repent or forfeit his life forever. That means I should turn from the silly preoccupations of my life and focus my mind's attention and my heart's affection on God and embrace Jesus Christ as my only hope for the forgiveness of my sins and for the hope of eternal life. That is God's message in the collapse of that bridge. This is his most merciful message: there is still time to turn from sin and unbelief and destruction for those of us who live. If we could see the eternal calamity he is offering escape from, we would hear this as the most precious message in the world.

Not long after we saw the news about the bridge, we prayed during our family devotions. Talitha (eleven years old), Noël, and I prayed earnestly for the families affected by the calamity and for the others in our city. Talitha prayed, "Please don't let anyone blame God for this but give thanks that they were saved."

When I sat on her bed and tucked her in and blessed her and sang over her, I said, "You know, Talitha, that was a good prayer, because when people blame God for something, they are angry with him, and they are saying that he has done something wrong. That's what *blame* means: to accuse somebody of wrongdoing. But you and I know that God did not do anything wrong. God always does what is wise. And you and I know that God could have held up that bridge with one hand." Talitha said, "With his pinky." "Yes," I said, "with his pinky, which means that God had a purpose for not holding up that bridge, knowing all that would happen, and he is infinitely wise in all that he wills."

Talitha said, "Maybe he let it fall because he wanted all the people of Minneapolis to fear him." "Yes, Talitha," I said, "I am sure that is one of the reasons God let the bridge fall."

I sang to her the song I always sing:

Come rest your head and nestle gently
And do not fear the dark of night.
Almighty God keeps watch intently,
And guards your life with all his might.
Doubt not his love, nor power to keep,
He never fails, nor does he sleep.

I said, "You know, Talitha, that is true whether you die in a bridge collapse or in a car accident or from cancer or terrorism or old age. God always keeps you, even when you die. So you don't need to be afraid, do you?" "No," she shook her head. I leaned down and kissed her. "Good night. I love you."

That night across the Twin Cities, families were wondering if they would ever kiss a loved one good night again. Some would not. I prayed that they would find Jesus Christ to be their Rock and Refuge in those agonizing hours of uncertainty and loss.

The word *bridge* does not occur in the Bible. There may be two reasons. One is that God doesn't build bridges; he divides seas. The other is that usually his people must pass through the deadly currents of suffering and death, not simply ride over them. "When you pass through the waters, I will be with you; and through the rivers, they shall not overwhelm you" (Isaiah 43:2). They may drown you. But I will be with you in life and death.

Who shall separate us from the love of Christ? Shall tribula-
tion, or distress, or persecution, or famine, or nakedness, or
danger, or sword? As it is written, "For your sake we are being
killed all the day long; we are regarded as sheep to be slaugh-

tered." No, in all these things we are more than conquerors through him who loved us. For I am sure that neither death nor life...will be able to separate us from the love of God in Christ Jesus our Lord. (Romans 8:35–39)

Killed all day long. But not separated from Christ. We go through the river, not over it. He went before us, crucified. He came out on the other side. He knows the way through. With him we will make it. That is the message we had that night, and still have, for the precious sinners in the Twin Cities. He died for your sins. He rose again. He saves all who trust him. We die, but because of him, we do not die.

Jesus said, "I am the resurrection and the life. Whoever believes in me, though he die, yet shall he live, and everyone who lives and believes in me shall never die" (John 11:25–26).

Talitha slept peacefully. I looked down on her with great love and thankfulness. But one day she will die. I teach her this. I will not always be there to bless her. But Jesus is alive and is the same yesterday, today, and forever. He will be with her because she trusts him. And she will make it through the river. And you will too, if you trust him. "When you pass through the waters, I will be with you; and through the rivers, they shall not overwhelm you" (Isaiah 43:2).

27

How the Cross Conquers Satan's Work

*God's Deliverance from God
as the Foundation of God's
Deliverance from Satan*

Satan's work is not the chief peril dealt with in the death of Christ. God's wrath is. God is opposed to us in his righteous wrath, and he is *for* us in his love. Therefore, in his great love, he sends his Son to endure his own wrath against us. In this way, his righteousness is upheld and his love is expressed. His wrath and curse and condemnation of our sin are endured for us by another—a substitute, Jesus Christ. Here are some of the texts that teach this:

- "Whoever believes in the Son has eternal life; whoever does not obey the Son shall not see life, but the *wrath of God* remains on him" (John 3:36).
- "Since…we have now been justified by his blood, much more shall we be saved by him from the *wrath of God*" (Romans 5:9).

- "[We] were by nature *children of wrath*.... But God... made us alive together with Christ" (Ephesians 2:3–5).
- "God has not destined us *for wrath,* but to obtain salvation through our Lord Jesus Christ who died for us" (1 Thessalonians 5:9-10).
- "Christ redeemed us from *the curse* of the law [which is an expression of his wrath] by becoming a curse for us [so that we do not bear God's wrath]" (Galatians 3:13).
- "By sending his own Son in the likeness of sinful flesh and for sin, [God] *condemned* sin in the flesh [thus, his wrathful condemnation of sin is expended on his Son's flesh, not ours]" (Romans 8:3).

Nevertheless, in dealing with God's wrath in this way, the double work of Satan is itself overcome. It is crucial that we see this wrath-bearing work of Christ as foundational to our deliverance from Satan's work. To say it more provocatively, it is crucial that we see our deliverance from God as foundational to our deliverance from Satan.

The double work of Satan is his work of *accusation* and his work of *temptation*. His name, Satan, means "accuser." And John described him that way, "The accuser of our brothers has been thrown down, who accuses them day and night before our God" (Revelation 12:10). And both Matthew and Paul called him "the tempter" (Matthew 4:3; 1 Thessalonians 3:5). Consider then how Christ's deliverance from the wrath of God is the foundation of his deliverance from both these works of Satan.

When Satan accuses us before God, what he accuses us with is sin. The only reason this accusation has a significance is that it is true. Both Satan and God know that we have sinned. And they both know that "the wages of sin is [eternal] death" (Romans 6:23). That is, God's appointed punishment for sin is eternal torment (Matthew 25:41, 46; Revelation 14:11). Sin deserves and receives God's wrath. "On account of these [sins] *the wrath of God* is coming" (Colossians 3:6). So Satan is laying claim to humans and saying that on God's own terms they must be damned like he is for his sin.

But at this point in Satan's accusation, Jesus Christ stands forth as our Advocate and intercedes for us. God designed this, desires this, and delights in this. "If anyone does sin, we have an advocate with the Father, Jesus Christ the righteous. He is the propitiation for our sins" (1 John 2:1–2). Christ's advocacy is based on his propitiation—his infallible securing of the removal of God's wrath for all who are in him. So Satan's accusations fall to the ground because our Advocate pleads his own blood and righteousness on our behalf. "Who is to condemn? Christ Jesus is the one who died—more than that, who was raised—who is at the right hand of God, who indeed is interceding for us" (Romans 8:34). Christ's advocacy and intercession for us nullify Satan's accusations against us. This advocacy and intercession are based on his death for us. By this death for us, Christ endured God's wrath against us. Therefore, Christ's deliverance from God's wrath is the foundation of his deliverance of us from Satan's accusations.

This is also true of our deliverance from Satan's temptations. Christ's propitiating work to deliver us from God's wrath is not only the foundation of our deliverance from Satan's accusations but also from his temptations. Many Christians fail to see this. That is why the gospel (the news of Christ's wrath-enduring, guilt-removing death and resurrection) is so often associated with starting the Christian life but not living the Christian life.

There are at least two ways that the New Testament shows how Christ's deliverance from God's wrath is the foundation for our deliverance from Satan's temptations. One is that our victory over Satan's temptations assumes God's merciful help by his Spirit. "Put on the whole armor of God, that you may be able to stand against the schemes of the devil" (Ephesians 6:11). "God may perhaps grant them repentance…and they may…escape from the snare of the devil" (2 Timothy 2:25–26). "By the Spirit you put to death the deeds of the body" (Romans 8:13).

Without the merciful gift of God's Spirit and the gift of God's armor and the gift of repentance, we cannot defeat the temptations of the devil. But the only reason God's full sanctifying mercy is flowing to us (through his Spirit and armor and repentance) is because his wrath isn't. And the reason his wrath isn't is because Christ endured it for us on the cross. Therefore, our deliverance from Satan's temptations is based on our deliverance from God's wrath.

One other way that the New Testament shows this is by teaching us that when Christ died for us, we died with him. And because we died with him, we can reckon ourselves dead to Satan's temptations to sin. "We have been united with [Christ] in a death like his…. Our old self was crucified with him in order that the body of sin might be brought to nothing, so that we would no longer be enslaved to sin" (Romans 6:5–6; see also Galatians 2:20). "One has died for all, therefore all have died" (2 Corinthians 5:14). Therefore, one of the ways we fight Satan's temptations to sin is to reckon ourselves dead to sin: "So you also must consider yourselves dead to sin and alive to God in Christ Jesus" (Romans 6:11). We can do this because when Christ died for us, we died in him.

But why did he have to die for us? Why did we have to die in him? Because the wages of sin is death. God's righteous wrath sooner or later falls on all sin (Colossians 3:6). Therefore, the death of Christ, by which we die to sin, is the same death that endures the wrath of God for us. The death that we die in Christ is both our punishment *for* sin and our death *to* sin. They are inseparable. That is why Christ's work to deliver us from the wrath of God is not only his deliverance from the accusations of the devil but also from the temptations of the devil.

Summarizing, Christ's wrath-enduring, propitiating work on the cross is the foundation of our justification *and* our sanctification. This justifying work of God corresponds to and conquers Satan's work of accusation. And this sanctifying work of God corresponds to and conquers Satan's work of temptation. In our justification, Satan's accusations lose their condemning power, and in our sanctification, Satan's temptations lose their corrupting power. And both—our deliverance from his accusations and our deliverance from his temptations—are based on our deliverance from God's wrath by the cross of Christ (that is, by his propitiation).

Therefore, in the defense of the gospel, let us never surrender the wrath-enduring substitution of Christ on our behalf. It is foundational to everything that matters in our lives. And in the radical living of the gospel for the glory of Christ and the good of the world, let us never get beyond the gospel of Christ crucified in our place. May it be our daily bread. May we live by its Satan-defeating power.

28

How Do You "Give" God Strength?

A Meditation on Psalm 96:7

Ponder with me the meaning of Psalm 96:7. All the modern versions translate it "Ascribe to the Lord...strength" (ESV, NIV, NASB). Only the King James Version renders it with the literal "*Give* unto the Lord...strength." The translation "ascribe" is surely legitimate. But we will go deeper on the way to that legitimacy if we ponder how one "gives" power to God.

There's nothing unusual about this Hebrew word *yahab*, or "give." It's used in the ordinary way the word *give* would be used. "*Give* your advice and counsel here" (Judges 20:7). "Oh *grant* us help against the foe" (Psalm 108:12). "The leech has two daughters: *Give* and *Give*" (Proverbs 30:15). "*Give* me my wife that I may go in to her" (Genesis 29:21).

"Ascribe" in Psalm 96:7 is an interpretation. It's a paraphrase. It's a good interpretation, I think, but, as with all paraphrases, it short-circuits our reflection. But for me, full-circuited reflection is where my soul gets its best food.

I start with the obvious. God is infinitely strong and cannot get stronger by my service. "[He is not] served by human hands, as though he needed anything" (Acts 17:25). So giving God strength stands for something different from adding to his strength. What then would be included in a full experience of what the psalmist means by "Give unto the Lord...strength."

First, by God's grace, we give attention to God and see that he is strong. We give heed to his strength. Then we give our approval to the greatness of his strength. We give due regard to its worth.

We find his strength to be wonderful. But what makes this wonder a "giving" kind of wonder is that we are especially glad that the greatness of the strength is his and not ours. We feel a profound fitness in the fact that he is infinitely strong and we are not. We love the fact that this is so. We do not envy God for his strength. We are not covetous of his power. We are full of joy that all strength is his. We are happy to *give* him all the credit for his power.

Everything in us rejoices to go out to behold this power, as if we had arrived at the celebration of the victory of a distance runner who had beaten us in the race, and we found our greatest joy in admiring his strength, rather than resenting our loss.

We find the deepest meaning in life when our hearts freely go out to admire God's power, rather than turning inward to boast of our own—or even think about our own. We discover something overwhelming: It is profoundly satisfying not to be God and to give up all thoughts or desires to be God.

In our giving heed to God's power there rises up in us a realization that God created the universe for this, so that we could have the supremely satisfying experience of not being God, but admiring the

Godness of God, the strength of God. There settles over us a peaceful realization that *admiration of the Infinite* is the final end of all things.

We tremble at the slightest temptation to claim any power as coming from us. God has made us weak to protect us from this: "We have this treasure in jars of clay, to show that the surpassing power belongs to God and not to us" (2 Corinthians 4:7).

O what love this is, that God would protect us from replacing the everlasting heights of admiring his power with the futile attempt to boast in our own.

God have mercy on me. Protect me from the suicidal desires for power. Awaken in me daily and ever more deeply the lowly will to give the gladdest and greatest assessment to your immeasurable strength. Forbid that I would sell the endless satisfaction of admiration for the mirage of my own strength.

In this sense, Lord, I give you strength. In this sense, I join the twenty-four elders in heaven and say, "Worthy are you, our Lord and God, to receive...power" (Revelation 4:11). Amen.

29

"He Will Rejoice over You with Gladness"

Why God Tells His Children That He Delights in Them

The question is not whether the triune God delights in his children. He does. The question is twofold: (1) What is it about us that he delights in? and (2) Why does he tell us this? What effect does he want it to have?

First, notice some of the texts that speak of God's delight in his people and his praise of them:

- "The LORD your God is in your midst, a mighty one who will save; *he will rejoice over you with gladness*" (Zephaniah 3:17).
- "*The Lord takes pleasure* in those who fear him, in those who hope in his steadfast love" (Psalm 147:11).
- "In this [salvation] you rejoice, though now for a little while, if necessary, you have been grieved by various trials, so that the tested genuineness of your faith—

more precious than gold that perishes though it is tested by fire—may be found to result in *praise and glory and honor* at the revelation of Jesus Christ" (1 Peter 1:6-7).

- "A Jew is one inwardly, and circumcision is a matter of the heart, by the Spirit, not by the letter. His *praise* is not from man but from God" (Romans 2:29).
- "Therefore do not pronounce judgment before the time, before the Lord comes, who will bring to light the things now hidden in darkness and will disclose the purposes of the heart. Then each one will receive his *commendation from God*" (1 Corinthians 4:5).

To answer the two questions we asked at the beginning, we also need to see the truth that God commands us to delight in him:

- "*Delight yourself in the* Lord, and he will give you the desires of your heart" (Psalm 37:4).
- "Then I will go to the altar of God, to *God my exceeding joy*" (Psalm 43:4).
- "Because your steadfast love is better than life, my lips will praise you" (Psalm 63:3).
- "May all who seek you *rejoice and be glad in you*! May those who love your salvation say evermore, 'God is great!'" (Psalm 70:4).
- "Through him we have also obtained access by faith into this grace in which we stand, and we *rejoice in hope of the glory of God*" (Romans 5:2).
- "*Rejoice in the Lord always;* again I will say, rejoice" (Philippians 4:4).

Notice that the Psalm 63 and 70 texts show something crucial. One says that when you love God's salvation you don't mainly say, "God's *salvation* is great!" You say, "*God* is great!" And when you experience the steadfast love of the Lord, you don't mainly say, "My lips will praise *your steadfast love.*" You mainly say, "My lips will praise *you*!"

In other words, in all these texts the command is to delight in God himself, and all other blessings we enjoy should lead us to God himself as our final and fullest satisfaction. Therefore, in answer to our first question, What is it about us that he delights in?, my answer is: *At root, what God delights in about us is that we delight in him.*

One way to get at this and show why it is true is to say the obvious: God approves of what is *right.* He rejoices in our thinking and feeling and doing what is right. But that leads to a crucial question: What is right, ultimately? What makes something right?

My answer is, rightness. That is, *thinking and feeling and acting in a way that expresses in true proportion the value of what is most valuable.* It seems manifestly wrong to ascribe highest value to what is not of highest value. And it seems manifestly right to ascribe highest value to what has highest value.

To put it more precisely: Rightness is thinking, feeling, and doing what flows from a true perception of the supreme value of God. It is seeing truly, savoring duly, and showing consistently in action the infinite worth of God. Therefore, we are doing what is right when we are *understanding* the truth of God's value for what it is, *feeling* it proportionately to his universal supremacy, and *acting* in ways that express God's supreme value. That is what "right" means.

Therefore, when we say God rejoices in our thinking and feeling and doing what is right, we mean that he delights in our seeing, savoring, and showing *his* own supreme value. God values our valuing him. That brings us back to our original suggestion: God delights in our delighting in him. God too must do what is right. His worth defines it.

Now the second question we asked is, Why does he tell us this? Should we be glad to hear it? Yes, we should be glad to hear it. But why? What is the bottom of our joy in hearing it? It is possible to hear it, and be glad to hear it, in a way that is devastating.

The proper reason to be glad that God delights in our delight in him is because *it confirms that our delight is truly in God.* This fixes our gaze more steadfastly on him and deepens our joy in his beauty.

But there is a devastating way to respond to God's commendation of us. What if we hear God's praise and are drawn away from delighting in God to delighting in God's delighting in us? What if we hear his praise as a tickler of what we really enjoy, namely, being made much of? What if the bottom line of what makes us happy is not God himself but God's attention, God's praise?

If that is the bottom line, then we are not delighting in God, but only using delight in God to get commendations. That would be devastating. When God's delight in us lures us to delight in being delighted in, we are ceasing to do the very thing God delights in.

The teaching that God delights in us is inescapably dangerous. The teaching is true. And the teaching is dangerous. The reason it is dangerous is that we are fallen, and the chief pleasure of our fallen nature is not sex but self-exaltation. Our sinful nature loves to be praised for what we are and what we have done.

The remedy for this is not to make God the praiser, and think all is well. All may not be well but deadly. God's praises of us will do us good if we hear them as confirming that we are truly delighting in him. God's praise of our delight in God is meant to help us keep on delighting in God and not be distracted by anything. God forbid that his praise of our delight in him would lead us away from delighting in him to delighting in being praised by him.

Hear me well. We *do* delight in being praised by God. But not the way a carnal mind would. God's praise of us is not the *bottom* of our joy. We should not let his praise distract us from the very thing he is praising—namely, our delight in him. *We delight in being praised by God because it confirms and increases our focus on him,* rather than distracting us from him. Even his merciful approval of our imperfect delight in him makes him more beautiful in himself. May those who hear the words, "Well done, good and faithful servant," say, "How great and merciful is our God!"

The relationship between what I have said here and the doctrine of justification by faith is that God looks upon his children through the lens of Christ's imputed righteousness. That means two things: (1) God counts us perfect in Christ, and (2) he can still see us becoming *in practice* what we are *positionally* in Christ.

The lens of imputation secures our invincible right standing with God. It also warrants God's delight in our imperfect delight in him. That is, even though we are counted perfectly righteous in Christ, God can still see our actual sinning mingled with the fruit of the Spirit in our life. That is why he can be delighted in us to greater or lesser degrees. We know this because he both reckons us as perfectly righteous (Romans 4:4-6) and disciplines us for sin in our life (1 Corinthians 11:32). Therefore, God's delight in our delight in him varies in proportion to the affections of our heart, but it is possible only be-cause God imputes to us Christ's perfect righteousness.

The upshot of all this is *Know your God.* Know his unsearchable excellence and supremacy. Savor what you know with all your heart. Admire fully the fully admirable. Enjoy deeply the infinitely enjoy-able. Marvel that he looks on your happy heart and delights in you. Give praise to Christ for making all this possible by becoming your perfection.

Caring Enough to Take the Risk

What to Say to the Depressed, Doubting, Skeptical, Confused, Angry

I f you care about people and risk talking to the depressed, the doubting, the skeptical, the confused, and the angry, you will soon run into a person who says to your counsel: *"I've tried that."* Whatever you say, they will minimize it and say it doesn't work. Do not be surprised at this response. This is what it means to be depressed, doubting, skeptical, confused, angry. It means that whatever they hear sounds useless.

So I want to offer some suggestions for what you say in a conversation that is about to be cut off like that.

1. Don't be offended.

First, resist the temptation to be offended. Don't pout or take your ball and go home. That's what you may feel like. They wanted to talk, and here they are throwing my suggestions back in my face with a dismissive attitude. Don't leave. Not yet. "Love is patient" (1 Corinthians 13:4).

2. Listen.

Next, listen to their responses. Part of your power is not only what you say but how they feel about the way you listen. If your truth produces empathetic ears, it will feel more compelling. This listening will be a witness. In 2 Timothy 2:24–26, Paul described the kind of engagement that may set people free from sin and error. One feature is "patiently enduring evil."

3. End with hope.

When you have spoken all the experiential counsel you can think of and they seem to have demeaned it all, don't let them have the last word of despair. You leave the last word of hope. The point is not to imitate these words but that you put hope-giving truth into their minds from God's Word, whether they think it is helpful or not. You might say something like this:

> I know you don't feel very helped by what I have said. I think I understand some of what that's like. I don't mean to be offering a quick fix, as though your problems or doubts can be turned around that easily. But I have more hope than you do at the moment that God's truth is powerful and will have its good effect in due time. May I share one more thing before you go?
>
> I simply want to make sure you hear the best news in the world. Jesus explained that the reason he spoke was so that we

would have peace (John 16:33). And Paul said that faith comes by hearing the word of Christ (Romans 10:17). You don't feel this right now. But God says peace and faith come from hearing.

Something happens. At one moment, you are not seeing Christ as beautiful and satisfying and compelling. Then in the next moment, you are. You don't see how this could happen. But it does.

In the moments leading up to this experience, listening to God's Word seems empty and futile. That doesn't put me off. If you doubt what I am saying, you are the very person who needs to hear what I am saying. It's the Word that does the work, not you.

So let me tell you some spectacular news. This comes from Colossians: "You, who were dead in your trespasses and the uncircumcision of your flesh, God made alive together with him, having forgiven us all our trespasses, by canceling the record of debt that stood against us with its legal demands. This he set aside, nailing it to the cross. He disarmed the rulers and authorities and put them to open shame, by triumphing over them in him" (Colossians 2:13–15).

There are five mind-blowing things here for you as God's child:

1. God makes you spiritually alive.
2. God forgives all your sins.
3. He does this because he canceled the record of debts that stood against you. You owed God what you could never pay because of all your sins. And he canceled the debt.

4. How could he do that? He set it aside by nailing it to the cross. But the nails that went into the cross didn't go through parchment. They went through Jesus' hands and feet. That's the heart of everything I have to say to you. Christ became our substitute and bore our debt.

5. When that happened, the devil was disarmed. Why? Because the weapon of accusation was taken out of his hand. He always waved that record of debt in our face and God's court. But now that's canceled. The devil is disarmed. He can huff and puff, but he cannot damn you.

I leave you with this news. I will pray that the obstacles to peace-filled faith in your mind will be overcome by these truths. Jesus said, "You will know the truth, and the truth will set you free" (John 8:32). Meditate on these verses. Remember it is the Word that does the work, not you.

Then pray out loud with and for them. *Lord of mercy and great patience, do your wonderful awakening, life-giving, hope-giving work by your word. In Jesus' name. Amen.*

31

Hero Worship and Holy Emulation

*Navigating the New World
of Media-Driven Celebrity*

I have unanswered questions about how to navigate the new world of media-driven celebrity attention to pastors. When I say media-driven attention, I am not mainly thinking about radio, TV, and newspapers. They are almost irrelevant. I mean Internet media. Most churches have websites. Sermons and articles and books are available. Often there's audio and video. And there's Facebook and Twitter. And by the time this book is in your hands, there will probably be some remarkable new development for putting your thoughts and your face before millions.

What happens then is that anywhere in the world people can read, watch, or listen. If they are helped, they can click and share it immediately with others anywhere in the world, who, in turn, share it again.

Tens of thousands of linkings may take place almost instantly—

through blogs, Twitter, texting, Facebook, and a dozen other sharing tools. This means that what a pastor does or says may be known in hours by hundreds of thousands of people around the world. This can contribute to media-driven celebrity status.

Then stir into the mix that some pastors write books. There is a popular mystique about authors. *Author* connotes authority or creativity or wisdom. Authors are generally thought to be interesting people. I think very often these conceptions are not true. But for some, the fact *that* an author writes is more significant than *what* he writes.

What is the meaning of the attention given to well-known pastors? What does the desire for autographs and photographs mean? The negative meaning would be something akin to name-dropping. Our egos are massaged if we can say we know someone famous. You see this on blogs with statements like "my friend Barack" and the like. And I presume that, for some, an autograph or a photo has the same ego boost.

However, I don't assume the worst of people. There are other possible motives. We will see this below. But it is good to emphasize that all of this is more dangerous to our souls than bullets and bombs. Pride is more fatal than death.

When I say "our souls" I mean all of us—the autograph seeker, the autograph giver, and the cynic who condemns it all. There is no escaping this new world of media technology. The question is, How do we navigate it for the glory of Christ—the crucifixion of self, the spreading of truth, the deepening of faith, and the empowering of sacrificial love?

Here is one small contribution. In spite of all the legitimate warnings against hero worship, I want to risk waving a flag for holy emulation, which includes realistic admiration. Hero worship means admiring someone for unholy reasons and seeing all he does as admirable (whether it's sin or not). Holy emulation, on the other hand, sees evidences of God's grace, and admires them for Christ's sake, and wants to learn from them and grow in them.

This theme is strong in the New Testament:

- "Be imitators of me, as I am of Christ" (1 Corinthians 11:1).
- "Brothers, join in imitating me, and keep your eyes on those who walk according to the example you have in us" (Philippians 3:17).
- "What you have learned and received and heard and seen in me—practice these things, and the God of peace will be with you" (Philippians 4:9).
- "And you became imitators of us and of the Lord" (1 Thessalonians 1:6).
- "You, however, have followed my teaching, my conduct, my aim in life, my faith, my patience, my love, my steadfastness" (2 Timothy 3:10).
- "Continue in what you have learned and have firmly believed, knowing from whom you learned it" (2 Timothy 3:14).
- "Show yourself in all respects to be a model of good works, and in your teaching show integrity, dignity" (Titus 2:7).
- "[Do] not be sluggish, but imitators of those who through faith and patience inherit the promises" (Hebrews 6:12).

The old Puritan Thomas Brooks commented on holy emulation in his book *The Secret Key to Heaven:*

> Bad men are wonderfully in love with bad examples.… Oh, that we were as much in love with the examples of good men as others are in love with the examples of bad men.
>
> Shall we love to look upon the pictures of our friends; and shall we not love to look upon the pious examples of those that are the lively and lovely picture of Christ? The pious examples of others should be the mirrors by which we should dress ourselves.
>
> He is the best and wisest Christian…that imitates those Christians that are most eminent in grace.… It is noble to live by the examples of the most eminent saints.*

It is right and risky to aim at being worthy of emulation. It is more foundationally right to aim at being helpful. It is essential in both that we be amazed that we are forgiven through Christ, and that we serve rather than seek to be served.

---

*Thomas Brooks, *The Secret Key to Heaven* (Edinburgh: Banner of Truth, 2006), 12–13.

32

Bless the Mother of Jesus—but Mainly Be the Mother of Jesus

Admiring the Imitable Mary

The veneration given to Mary in the Roman Catholic Church is beyond what is warranted by the New Testament. In fact, it is astonishing how little we see of Mary in the New Testament. Let us honor her unique motherhood. Let us count her blessed as the mother of our incarnate Lord. But let us not put her on a pedestal that neither she nor Jesus would have approved of.

After she turns up with the disciples praying in the upper room in Acts 1:14, she is never mentioned again in the New Testament. This is astonishing to anyone who thinks that the veneration of Mary was an essential part of early church life. It was not important enough to be mentioned in any of the New Testament books after Acts.

In fact, in the one place where Paul came close to mentioning Mary, he chose not to, and simply used the generic "woman": "When the fullness of time had come, God sent forth his Son, born of woman" (Galatians 4:4).

And when she is mentioned in Acts 1:14, she is "Mary the mother of Jesus, and his brothers." This inclusion of the brothers has the effect of minimizing any emerging elevation of Mary as having significance only in being the mother of Jesus, rather than the mother of his brothers as well.

Mary is unique among all women in being a virgin when she gave birth to her firstborn son. "Behold, the virgin shall conceive and bear a son" (Matthew 1:23). When she asked the angel how that could be, he answered, "The Holy Spirit will come upon you, and the power of the Most High will overshadow you; therefore the child to be born will be called holy—the Son of God" (Luke 1:35).

Yet amazingly, the virgin birth of Jesus by Mary is never mentioned again in the New Testament. That doesn't mean it is untrue or unimportant. It simply means that it was not prominent in the life of the church. Celebrating it was not an essential part of the worship of the New Testament church. Otherwise, it would have been mentioned somewhere in the letters to those churches.

When Mary is referred to during the adult life of Jesus in the Gospels, she is not treated in a way that sets her apart in any unusual way. At the cross, for example, Matthew referred to her without even mentioning that she was Jesus' mother: "There were also many women there, looking on from a distance, who had followed Jesus from Galilee, ministering to him, among whom were Mary Magdalene and Mary the mother of James and Joseph and the mother of the sons of Zebedee" (Matthew 27:55–56).

Calling Jesus' mother "the mother of James and Joseph" is striking. We know that this is Jesus' mother because of Matthew 13:55: "Is not his mother called Mary? And are not his brothers James and

Joseph and Simon and Judas?" "James and Joseph" are the sons in both Matthew 27:56 and 13:55. So Matthew referred to Mary without calling her the mother of Jesus, and a few verses later he simply referred to her as "the other Mary" (27:61).

Most striking of all is the way Jesus intentionally deflected a certain kind of honor from his mother. Once a woman in the crowd "raised her voice and said to him, 'Blessed is the womb that bore you, and the breasts at which you nursed!'" But Jesus replied, "Blessed rather are those who hear the word of God and keep it!" (Luke 11:27–28). Jesus ranks obedience to the Word of God above the special veneration of his mother.

Similarly, Jesus was once told, "Your mother and your brothers are standing outside, desiring to see you." But Jesus answered, "My mother and my brothers are those who hear the word of God and do it" (Luke 8:20–21). Again Jesus ranks obedience above the standing of his mother.

Mary was a magnificent person.

- Her humility shone: "He has looked on the humble estate of his servant" (Luke 1:48).
- Her faith was profound: "Blessed is she who believed that there would be a fulfillment of what was spoken to her from the Lord" (Luke 1:45).
- Her suffering was deep: "A sword will pierce through your own soul" (Luke 2:35).
- Her God was sovereign: "He has shown strength with his arm; he has scattered the proud in the thoughts of their hearts; he has brought down the mighty from their thrones" (Luke 1:51–52).

- And her meditations were full of truth: "Mary treasured up all these things, pondering them in her heart" (Luke 2:19).

Therefore, remember her. Admire her. Bless her. Be inspired by her. But do not go beyond what the New Testament portrays. Our calling is to *be* the mother of Jesus more than to venerate her. "My mother is the one who hears the word of God and does it" (Luke 8:21).

33

How the Lord of Life Gives Life

A Meditation on Acts 16:14

It seems that everywhere Paul preached some believed and some did not. How are we to understand why some of those who are "dead in trespasses and sins" (Ephesians 2:1) believed and some did not?

One answer why some did not believe is that they "thrust it aside" (Acts 13:46) because the message of the gospel was "folly to [them], and [they were] not able to understand" (1 Corinthians 2:14). The mind of the flesh "is hostile to God, for it does not submit to God's law; indeed, it cannot" (Romans 8:7). Those who hear and reject the gospel "[hate] the light" and do not come to the light lest their deeds should be exposed (John 3:20). They remain "darkened in their understanding...because of the ignorance that is in them, due to their hardness of heart" (Ephesians 4:18). It is a guilty ignorance. The truth is available. But "by their unrighteousness [they] suppress the truth" (Romans 1:18).

But why then do some believe, since all are in this condition of rebellious hardness of heart, dead in our trespasses? The book of Acts gives the answer in at least three different ways. One is that they are appointed to believe. When Paul preached in Antioch of Pisidia, the Gentiles rejoiced and "as many as were appointed to eternal life believed" (Acts 13:48).

Another way of answering why some believe is that God granted repentance. When the saints in Jerusalem heard that Gentiles were responding to the gospel and not just Jews, they said, "Then to the Gentiles also God has granted repentance that leads to life" (Acts 11:18).

But the clearest answer in Acts to the question why a person believes the gospel is that God opens the heart. Lydia is the best example. Why did she believe? Acts 16:14 says, "The Lord opened her heart to pay attention to what was said by Paul." Notice four aspects of this conversion—four things necessary for a person to believe and be saved.

1. "What was said by Paul." First, someone must speak the gospel. God does not open the eyes of the heart to see nothing. He opens them to see the glory of Christ in the truth of the gospel (2 Corinthians 4:4–6). Therefore, we must speak the gospel. We don't make the new birth happen when we do. But we fit into God's way of doing it. The point of the new birth is to grant spiritual sight. The point of speaking the gospel is so that an unbeliever has something to see when God opens the eyes. New birth—the miracle that enables faith (1 John 5:1)—is for the glory of Christ. Therefore, God causes it to happen when Christ is lifted up.

2. "The Lord." Next, the speaker of the gospel relies upon the Lord. Prayer is not mentioned here. But that is what we do when we realize that it is the Lord who is the decisive actor, not us. We have a significant role in speaking the gospel, but it is the Lord himself who does the decisive work.

3. "**Opened her heart.**" Since the key problem in not believing the gospel is the hardness, or the *closedness,* of the heart, this is where the Lord does his decisive work. He "opens the heart" of Lydia. This means he takes out the heart of stone and puts in the heart of flesh (Ezekiel 36:26). God says with sovereign authority, "Let there be light," and "[shines] in our hearts to give the light of the knowledge of the glory of God in the face of Jesus Christ" (2 Corinthians 4:6). So the darkness flies away and the light of truth reveals the beauty of Christ in the gospel as irresistibly compelling.

4. "**To pay attention to what was said by Paul.**" The effect of the Lord's opening Lydia's heart is a true spiritual hearing of the gospel. "Pay attention to" is a weak translation of the Greek *prosechein.* It is stronger than that in this context. In this verse, it is a hearing with attachment. The work of the Lord does not just help Lydia focus. It brings about faith. She was granted repentance (2 Timothy 2:25) and faith (Philippians 1:29).

Or, in the terms of John 6, she was given by the Father to the Son (v. 37), and was drawn by the Father to the Son (v. 44), and was granted by the Father to come to the Son (v. 65). She was made alive (Ephesians 2:5) and was born again (John 3:3, 7).

This is what we should pray for. When God does this for many at the same time in the same area, we have historically called it "revival." It is the great need of our day, as every day. As the old gospel song says, "Mercy drops around us are falling, but for the showers we plead"— showers of the kind of spiritual awakening Lydia received.

34

Awakened by Suffering and Pain

*Abraham Lincoln's Path
to Divine Providence*

Into his forties, Abraham Lincoln remained skeptical, and at times even cynical, about religion. But it is remarkable how, as time went by, personal and national suffering drew Lincoln into the reality of God, rather than pushing him away.

In 1862, when Lincoln was fifty-three years old, his eleven-year-old son, Willie, died. Lincoln's wife tried to deal with her grief by searching out New Age mediums. Lincoln turned to Phineas Gurley, pastor of the New York Avenue Presbyterian Church in Washington, DC. Several long talks led to what Gurley described as "a conversion to Christ." Lincoln confided that he was "driven many times upon my knees by the overwhelming conviction that I have nowhere else to go."

Similarly, the horrors of the dead and wounded soldiers assaulted him daily. There were fifty hospitals for the wounded in Washington. The rotunda of the Capitol held 2,000 cots for wounded soldiers.

Typically, fifty soldiers a day died in these temporary hospitals. All of this drove Lincoln deeper into the providence of God. "We cannot but believe, that He who made the world still governs it."

His most famous statement about the providence of God in relation to the Civil War was in his second inaugural address, given a month before he was assassinated. It is remarkable for his not making God a simple supporter for the Union or Confederate cause. God has his own purposes and does not excuse sin on either side:

> Fondly do we hope—fervently do we pray—that this mighty scourge of war might speedily pass away.... Yet if God wills that it continue, until all the wealth piled by the bond-man's two hundred years of unrequited toil shall be sunk, and until every drop of blood drawn with the lash, shall be paid with another drawn with the sword, as was said three thousand years ago so still it must be said, "the judgments of the Lord, are true and righteous altogether."

The paradoxical words of Alexander Solzhenitsyn eighty years later, whose imprisonment in Joseph Stalin's "corrective labor camps" led not to despair but to the discovery of goodness, would have resonated with Lincoln:

> It was granted to me to carry away from my prison years on my bent back, which nearly broke beneath its load, this essential experience: how a human being becomes evil and how good. In the intoxication of youthful successes I had felt myself to be infallible, and I was therefore cruel. In the surfeit of

power I was a murderer and an oppressor. In my most evil moments I was convinced that I was doing good, and I was well supplied with systematic arguments. It was only when I lay there on rotting prison straw that I sensed within myself the first stirrings of good. Gradually it was disclosed to me that the line separating good and evil passes not through states, nor between classes, nor between political parties either—but right through every human heart—and through all human hearts.… That is why I turn back to the years of my imprisonment and say, sometimes to the astonishment of those about me: *"Bless you, prison!"* I…have served enough time there. I nourished my soul there, and I say without hesitation: *"Bless you, prison,* for having been in my life!"*

As I write this I am praying for you the reader—you who sooner or later will suffer loss and injury and great sorrow. I pray that it will awaken for you, as it did for Lincoln and Solzhenitsyn not an empty nihilism, but a deeper reliance on the infinite wisdom and love of God's inscrutable providence. "Oh, the depth of the riches and wisdom and knowledge of God! How unsearchable are his judgments and how inscrutable his ways!" (Romans 11:33).

---

*Alexander Solzhenitsyn, *The Gulag Archipelago: 1918–1956,* (New York: Harper & Row, 1974), 615–17.

35

The Strange Task of Witnessing About Light

A Meditation on John 1:7

Witnessing about light is a strange task if your aim is for people to see the light and believe in the light. Light illumines by itself. When you want someone to see a light, do you talk about the light? You hold up the light. If you have a torch in your hand, and you want someone to see the torch, you don't say, "This is a torch." You hold up the torch.

But John 1:7 says that John the Baptist "came as a witness, to bear witness about the light." So as strange as this task is, that was John's mission. And it is ours too. So then, what do we learn about our task when it is described as witnessing to the light?

1. We learn that Christ, the Light of the world (John 8:12), shines not like a physical torch before the physical eye but like a spiritual glory before the spiritual eye. This is why Jesus said, "Seeing they do not see" (Matthew 13:13). And it is why Paul prayed that you would have "the eyes of your hearts enlightened, that you may know what is the hope to which he has called you" (Ephesians 1:18). There is a seeing that we do with "the eyes of the heart," not merely with the eyes of the head.

2. We learn that the light of Christ, this spiritual glory which we see with the eyes of the heart, shines mainly through a message—the gospel. That is, it shines mainly through the witness of human beings, about what Jesus accomplished when he died and rose again. This is strange—strange and wonderful. Light shines through words. Yes it does. Paul said:

> The god of this world has blinded the minds of the unbelievers, to keep them from seeing *the light of the gospel of the glory of Christ,* who is the image of God.... God, who said, "Let light shine out of darkness," has shone in our hearts to give *the light of the knowledge of the glory of God in the face of Jesus Christ.* (2 Corinthians 4:4–6)

The glory of Christ is his light. This glory, Paul said, shines as "the light of the gospel." That means it shines through a *witness.* When we witness to what Christ achieved for us in dying, we are *witnessing about the light.* That is how the light of Christ shines in this world. Deeds of love are crucial in this shining (Matthew 5:14–16). But deeds alone cannot witness effectually to the greatest glory of Christ, namely, his achievement on the cross. That light shines through the gospel in the mouths of witnesses.

3. We learn that people need to have the eyes of their hearts opened to see the light of Christ in the gospel. Jesus said to Paul when he sent him to witness to the light, "I am sending you to *open their eyes,* so that they may turn from darkness to light and from the power of Satan to God, that they may receive forgiveness of sins" (Acts 26:17–18).

God does this eye-opening work through human witnesses. The book of Luke tells us that the way Lydia saw the light was that "the Lord opened her heart to pay attention to what was said by Paul" (Acts 16:14). Paul witnessed to the light. God opened her heart to see the light. So Paul prays that this would happen: "I do not cease to give thanks for you, remembering you in my prayers, that...[you would have] the eyes of your hearts enlightened" (Ephesians 1:16–18). God's answer to that prayer is described in 2 Corinthians 4:6: "[God] has shone in our hearts to give the light of the knowledge of the glory of God in the face of Jesus Christ."

So we witness about the light, even though we know that people are blind to this light. But that does not daunt us, because we know that God's eye-opening power accompanies the witness about his Son. This is why the Holy Spirit was given. As Jesus said, "He will glorify me" (John 16:14).

4. We learn that the miracle of spiritual sight through the gospel happens when witnesses tell blind people to look at Christ and then describe what they will see when they look there. There is a mental analogy to this spiritual reality. Consider a typical optical illusion like the one on the facing page.

Suppose someone only sees one picture in this illustration. They are "blind" to the other. Then you "witness" to them: "Look at this. There are two pictures: a girl's face and a man playing a saxophone." That very witness opens their eyes to both pictures.

It's only an analogy, because in the spiritual realm the process is not merely mental or natural. It is spiritual and supernatural. But we

can get some idea of how it is possible to be spiritually blind and yet God can use a witness to open our eyes.

Therefore, don't let the strangeness of witnessing about light stop you. It is gloriously strange. It is strange in a way that gives us hope that we really can help the blind to see. It is strange in a way that will get all the glory for God—*both* in the gospel itself and in the way people see the glory of Christ in it.

36

Submission and Headship in the Home Where I Grew Up

Female Competency and Biblical Complementarity

My mother and father were unusually clear examples of headship and submission in its happiest, healthiest form. What made it so illuminating in retrospect was that my mother's submissive role in relation to my father's was not owing to lesser competencies. Nor was it demanded, coerced, or abused by my father. It was owing to the God-given nature of manhood and womanhood and how they are designed in marriage to display the covenant relationship between Christ and the church.

I grew up in a home where my father was away for about two-thirds of each year. He was an evangelist. He held about twenty-five evangelistic crusades each year ranging in length from one to three weeks. He would leave on Saturday, be gone for one to three weeks, and come home on a Monday afternoon. In my eighteen years growing up in this home, I went to the Greenville airport hundreds of times. And some of the sweetest memories of my childhood include the smile on my father's face as he came out of the plane and down the steps and almost ran across the runway to hug and kiss me (no jetways in those days).

This meant that my sister and I were reared and trained mostly by my mother. She taught me almost everything practical that I know. She taught me how to cut the grass (overlap enough so you don't miss any), how to keep a checkbook and ride a bike, how to drive a car, make notes for a speech, set the table with the fork in the right place, and make pancakes (notice when the bubbles form on the edges). She paid the bills, handled repairs, cleaned house, cooked meals, helped me with my homework, took us to church, led us in devotions. She was superintendent of the intermediate youth department at church, head of the community garden club, and tireless doer of good for others.

She was incredibly strong in her loneliness. The early sixties were the days in Greenville, South Carolina, when civil rights were in the air. The church took a vote one Wednesday night on a resolution to not allow black people to worship in our church. When the vote was taken, she stood, as I recall, entirely alone in opposition. And when my sister was married in the church in 1963 and one of the ushers tried to seat some black friends of our family all alone in the balcony, my mother indignantly marched out of the sanctuary and seated them herself on the main floor with everyone else.

I have never known anyone quite like Ruth Piper. She seemed to me to be omnicompetent and overflowing with love and energy.

But here is my point. When my father came home, my mother

had the extraordinary ability and biblical wisdom and humility to honor him as the head of our home. She was, in the best sense of the word, submissive to him. In fact, it was manifest even to a child that she loved the homecoming of my father and the relief of his leadership. This was not a sacrifice for her to submit to his leading. It was a burden lifted. It was an amazing thing to watch week after week as my father came and went. He went, and my mother ruled the whole house with a firm and competent and loving hand. And he came home, and my mother deferred to his leadership.

Once he was home, he was the one who prayed at the meals. It was he who led in devotions. It was he who drove us to worship, watched over us in the pew, and answered our questions. My fear of disobedience shifted from my mother's wrath to my father's, for there too he took the lead. Their preciousness and the overwhelming dominance of their happy smiles made their disapproval all the worse.

I never heard my father attack my mother or put her down in any way. They sang together and laughed together and put their heads together to bring each other up to date on the state of the family. The happy complementarity of Ruth and Bill Piper was a gift of God that I could never begin to repay or earn.

And here is what I learned: a biblical truth before I knew it was in the Bible. There is no correlation between submission and incompetence. There is such a thing as masculine leadership that does not demean a wife. There is such a thing as submission that is not weak or mindless or manipulative.

It never entered my mind until I began to hear feminist rhetoric in the late sixties that this beautiful design in my home was somehow owing to anyone's inferiority. It wasn't. It was owing to this: My mother and my father put their hope in God and believed that obedience to his Word would create the best of all possible families. I am thankful. And I exhort you with all my heart to consider these things with great seriousness, and do not let the world squeeze you into its mold.

37

When Signs and Wonders Go Bad

*Reflections on Heresy, Deception,
and Love for God*

Does God have designs for deceptive signs and wonders? Does he have purposes for heresies?

From the time of Moses to the end of history, this has been and will be an issue. Jesus promised that "false christs and false prophets will arise and perform *great signs and wonders,* so as to lead astray, if possible, even the elect" (Matthew 24:24). These are not little tricks. They are *great* signs and wonders. Great. But aimed to deceive.

Paul said that "the coming of the lawless one is by the activity of Satan with all power and *false signs and wonders,* and with all wicked deception for those who are perishing, because they refused to love the truth and so be saved" (2 Thessalonians 2:9–10). "False signs and wonders" is a literal translation to show that the falseness of the signs and wonders is not that they aren't real miracles, but that they lie about reality. They are real miracles, and they lead away from Christ.

Similarly, to the end of history—*especially* at the end of history—false teaching and heresies will dog the church. "The time is coming when people will not endure sound teaching, but having itching ears they will accumulate for themselves teachers to suit their own passions, and will turn away from listening to the truth and wander off into myths" (2 Timothy 4:3–4).

At the other end of history, things have been this way from the time of Moses. And it is Moses who answers our two questions: Does God have designs for deceptive signs and wonders? Does he have purposes for heresies? He does. Here's the key passage:

> If a prophet or a dreamer of dreams arises among you and gives you a sign or a wonder, and the sign or wonder that he tells you comes to pass, and if he says, "Let us go after other gods," which you have not known, "and let us serve them," you shall not listen to the words of that prophet or that dreamer of dreams. For the LORD your God is testing you, to know whether you love the LORD your God with all your heart and with all your soul. (Deuteronomy 13:1–3)

Notice five things:

First, Moses tells us that signs and wonders in the service of heresy really happen. They are not tricks. "If a prophet...gives you a sign or a wonder, and the sign or wonder that he tells you comes to pass..." (v. 1). They really do come to pass. It is not smoke and mirrors. These are supernatural but not in the service of truth.

Second, some miracle workers aim to draw believers away from the true God. "If he says, 'Let us go after other gods...' you shall not listen to the words of that prophet" (vv. 2–3). In other words, some heresies ("let us go after other gods") are endorsed with miraculous signs and wonders.

Third, God has a design in these deceptive signs and wonders, and he has purposes for the heresies they support. He mentions one of these designs and purposes: "For the LORD your God is testing you, to know whether you love the LORD your God with all your heart and with all your soul" (v. 3). When temptation happens from man, a test is happening from God. This is God's design in the deceptive signs and heresies.

Fourth, your love for God is what God is testing. "Your God is testing you, to know whether you love the LORD your God with all your heart and with all your soul" (v. 3).

Fifth, I conclude from this that the heart that loves God sees through miraculous deception. It is not deluded. Love for God is not based mainly on miraculous power. It is based on seeing through miraculous power to true divine beauty. Therefore, love for God is a powerful protection against heresy, even when it comes with miraculous confirmation.

Understanding these five things from Deuteronomy 13:1–3 helps protect us from deceptive signs and wonders and from heresies. But understanding is not enough. Love for God is both the aim of God's testing and the means by which his tests are passed. Understanding awakens us to our need to love him. But love for God sees through deceptive signs and wonders to the falsehood they support and flees to Christ. Love for God sees through the heresy and holds fast to him.

Recall 2 Thessalonians 2:10 from above. People are swept into the satanic delusion "because they refused to *love* the truth." It isn't just *knowing* truth that protects us; it's *loving* it. Because *it* reveals *him*—our God, our all-surpassing Treasure and Refuge.

May God deepen our love for him so that it has this kind of penetrating, protecting power.

38

Coed Combat and Cultural Cowardice

Why Women Suffer as Chivalry Collapses

I f I were the last man on the planet to think so, I would want the honor of saying that no woman should go before me into combat to defend my country. A man who endorses women in combat is not pro-woman; he's acting like a wimp. He should be ashamed. For most of history, in most cultures, he would have been utterly scorned as a coward to promote such an idea. Part of the meaning of manhood as God created us is the sense of responsibility for the safety and welfare of our women.

Back in the seventies, when I taught in college, feminism was new and cool. So my ideas on manhood were viewed as the social construct of a dying chauvinistic era. I had not yet been enlightened that competencies, not divine wiring, governed the roles we assume. Unfazed, I said no. I still say no.

Suppose I said to a class one day, a couple of you students, Jason and Sarah, were walking to McDonald's after dark. And suppose a man with a knife jumped out of the bushes and threatened you. And suppose Jason knows that Sarah has a black belt in karate and could probably disarm the assailant better than he could. Should he step back and hope she would do it? No. He should step in front of her and be ready to lay down his life to protect her, irrespective of competency. It is written on his soul. That is what manhood does.

And collectively that is what society does, unless the men have all been emasculated by the self-destructive songs of egalitarian folly. God created man first in order to say that man bears a primary burden for protection, provision, and leadership. And when man and woman rebelled against God's ways, God came to the garden and said, "Adam, where are you?" (Genesis 3:9), not "Eve, where are you?" And when the apostle described the implications of being created male and female, the pattern he celebrates is: Save her, nourish her, cherish her, give her life (Ephesians 5:25–29).

God wrote manhood and womanhood on our hearts. Sin ruins the imprint without totally defacing it. It tells men to be heavy-handed oafs or passive wimps. It tells women to be coquettes or controllers. That is not God's imprint. Deeper down, men and women know it.

When God is not in the picture, the truth crops up in strange forms. For example, Kingsley Browne, law professor at Wayne State University in Michigan, wrote a book called *Co-ed Combat: The New Evidence That Women Shouldn't Fight the Nation's Wars*. In an interview with *Newsweek* he said, "The evidence comes from the field of evolutionary psychology.... Men don't say, 'This is a person I would follow through the gates of hell.' Men aren't hard-wired to follow women into danger."*

---

*Martha Brant, "The Case Against Women in Combat," *Newsweek,* October 23, 2007. www.newsweek.com/id/61568.

If you leave God out, the perceived hard-wiring appears to be evolutionary psychology. If God is in the picture, it has other names. We call it "the work of the law...written on their hearts" (Romans 2:15). We call it true manhood as God meant it to be.

As usual, the truth that comes in the alien form of evolutionary psychology gets distorted. It is true that "men aren't hard-wired to follow women into danger." But that's misleading. The issue is not that women are leading men into danger. The issue is, they are leading men. Men aren't hard-wired to follow women, period. They are hard-wired to get in front of their women—between them and the bullets. They are hard-wired to lead their women out of danger and into safety. And women, at their deepest and most honest selves, give profound assent to this noble impulse in good men. That is why coed combat situations compromise men and women at their core and corrupt even further the foolhardy culture that put them there.

Consider where we have come. One promotion for Browne's book states, "More than 155,000 female troops have been deployed to Iraq and Afghanistan since 2002. And more than seventy of those women have died.... Those deaths exceed the number of military women who died in Korea, Vietnam, and the Gulf War combined."

What cowardly men do we thank for this collapse of chivalry? Browne suggests, "There are a lot of military people who think women in combat is a horrible idea, but it's career suicide to say it." In other words, let the women die; I'll keep my career. May God restore sanity and courage once again to our leading national defenders. And may he give you a voice.

39

Why Require Unregenerate Children to Act Like They're Good?

Three Reasons for Parenting by God's Revealed Will

If mere external conformity to God's commands (like don't lie, don't steal, don't kill) is hypocritical and spiritually defective, then why should parents require obedience from their unregenerate children? Won't this simply confirm them in unspiritual religious conformity, hypocritical patterns of life, and legalistic moralism?

Here are at least three reasons why Christian parents should require their small children (regenerate or unregenerate) to behave in ways that conform externally to God's revealed will.

I say "small children" because as a child gets older, there are certain external conformities to God's revealed will that should be required and others that should not. It seems to me, for example, while parents should require drug-free, respectful decency from a fifteen-year-old, it would do little good to require an unbelieving, indifferent, angry fifteen-year-old to read his Bible every day. But it would be wise to require that of a six-year-old, while doing all they can to help him enjoy it and see the benefit in it. Where to draw this line is a matter of wisdom.

So the following points are reasons why we should require younger children to behave in ways that conform, at least externally, to God's Word.

1. For children, external, unspiritual conformity to God's commanded patterns of behavior is better than external, unspiritual nonconformity to those patterns of behavior.

A respectful and mannerly five-year-old unbeliever is better for the world than a more authentic defiant, disrespectful, ill-mannered, unbelieving bully. The family, the friendships, the church, and the world in general will be thankful for parents who restrain the egocentric impulses of their children and confirm in them every impulse toward courtesy and kindness and respect.

2. Requiring obedience from children in conformity with God's will confronts them with the meaning of sin in relation to God, the nature of their own depravity, and their need for inner transformation by the power of grace through the gospel of Christ.

There comes a point where the "law" dawns on the child. That is, he realizes that God (not just his parents) requires a certain way of life from him and that he does not like some of it and that he cannot do all of it.

At this crisis moment, the good news of Christ's dying for our sins becomes all important. Will the child settle into a moralistic effort the rest of his life, trying to win the acceptance and love of God? Or will he hear and believe that God's acceptance and forgiveness and love are free gifts, and then receive this God in Christ as the supreme Treasure of his life?

The child will have a hard time grasping the meaning of the Cross if parents have not required of him behaviors, some of which he dislikes, and none of which he can do perfectly.

Christ lived and died to provide for us the righteousness we need (but cannot perform) and to endure for us the punishment we deserve (but cannot endure). If parents do not require external righteousness and apply measures of punishment, the categories of the Cross will be difficult for a child to grasp.

3. The marks of devotion, civility, and manners ("please," "thank you," and good eye contact) are habits that, God willing, are filled later with grace and become more helpful ways of blessing others and expressing a humble heart.

No parents have the luxury of teaching their child nothing while they wait for his regeneration. If we are not requiring obedience, we are confirming defiance. If we are not inculcating manners, we are training in boorishness. If we are not developing the disciplines of prayer and Bible-listening, we are solidifying the sense that prayerlessness and Biblelessness are normal.

Inculcated good habits may later become formalistic legalism. Inculcated insolence, rudeness, and irreligion will likely become worldly decadence. But by God's grace, and saturated with parental prayer, good habits may be filled with the life of the Spirit by faith.

But the patterns of insolence and rudeness and irreligion will be hard to undo.

Caution: Here we are only answering one question. Why should parents require submissive behaviors of children when they may be unregenerate rebels at heart? Of course, that is not all Christian parents should do.

- Let us spontaneously celebrate verbally every hopeful sign of life and goodness in our children.
- Let us express forgiveness often and be long-suffering.
- Let us apologize often when we fall short of our own Father's requirements.
- Let us serve them and not use them.
- Let us lavish them with joyful participation in their interests.
- Let us model for them the joy of knowing and submitting to the Lord Jesus.
- Let us pray for them without ceasing.
- Let us saturate them with the Word of God from the moment they are in the womb (the uterus is not soundproof).
- Let us involve them in happy ministry experiences and show them it is more blessed to give than to receive.
- Let them see us sing to the King.
- Let us teach them relentlessly the meaning of the gospel in the hope that God will open their eyes and make them alive. It happens through the gospel (1 Peter 1:22–25).

Each of those points deserves a chapter. But the point here is narrower: When children are small they are being taught by us, even if we do nothing (which we never do). We should not fear requiring of them external behaviors in accord with God's Word from the time they can process any command. We are not making hypocrites out of them; we are preparing them for the gospel and for a fruitful life.

40

"Do Good to Everyone"

*If God Wills Disease, Why Should
We Try to Eradicate It?*

The question arises from biblical teaching, are all things ultimately under God's control? Scripture answers it this way: "My
counsel shall stand, and I will accomplish all my purpose" (Isaiah
46:10). "Whatever the LORD pleases, he does, in heaven and on earth,
in the seas and all deeps" (Psalm 135:6). "He does according to his
will among the host of heaven and among the inhabitants of the earth;
and none can stay his hand or say to him, 'What have you done?'"
(Daniel 4:35). "[He] works all things according to the counsel of his
will" (Ephesians 1:11).

This means that God governs all calamity and all disease. Satan
is real and has a hand in it, but he is not ultimate and can do nothing
but what God permits (Job 1:12–2:10). And God does not permit
things willy-nilly. He permits things for a reason. There is infinite
wisdom in all he does and all he permits. So what he permits is part of
his plan just as much as what he does more directly.

Therefore this raises the question, if God wills disease, why should we try to eradicate it? This is a crucial question for me because I have heard Christians say that believing in the sovereignty of God hinders Christians from working hard to eradicate diseases like malaria and tuberculosis and cancer and AIDS.

They think the logic goes like this: If God sovereignly wills all things, including malaria, then we would be striving against God to invest millions of dollars to find a way to wipe it out.

That is not the logic the Bible teaches. And it is not what lovers of God's sovereignty have historically believed. In fact, lovers of God's sovereignty have been among the most aggressive scientists who have helped subdue creation and bring it under the dominion of man for his good, just like Psalm 8:6 says, "You have given [man] dominion over the works of your hands; you have put all things under his feet."

The logic of the Bible says to act according to God's "will of command," not according to his "will of decree." God's will of decree is whatever comes to pass. "If the Lord wills, we will live and do this or that" (James 4:15). God's "will of decree" ordained that his Son be betrayed (Luke 22:22), ridiculed (Isaiah 53:3), mocked (Luke 18:32), flogged (Matthew 20:19), forsaken (Matthew 26:31), pierced (John 19:37), and killed (Mark 9:31). But the Bible teaches us plainly that we *should not* betray, ridicule, mock, flog, forsake, pierce, or kill innocent people. That is God's will of command. We do not look at the death of Jesus, clearly willed by God, and conclude that killing Jesus is good and that we should join the mockers.

In the same way, we do not look at the devastation of malaria or AIDS and conclude that we should join the ranks of the indifferent. No. "Love your neighbor" is God's will of command (Matthew 22:39). "Do to others as you would have them do to you" is God's will of command (Matthew 7:12, NIV). "If your enemy is hungry, feed him" is God's will of command (Romans 12:20). The disasters that God ordains are not aimed at paralyzing his people with indifference but mobilizing them with compassion.

When Paul taught that "the creation was subjected to futility," he also taught that this subjection was "in hope that the creation itself will be set free from its bondage to corruption and obtain the freedom of the glory of the children of God" (Romans 8:20–21). There is no reason that Christians should not embrace this futility-lifting calling now. God will complete it in the age to come. But it is a good thing to conquer as much disease and suffering now, in the name of Christ, as we can.

In fact, I would wave the banner right now and call some of you who are reading this to enter vocations of research that may be the means of undoing some of the great diseases of the world. This is not fighting against God. God is as much in charge of the research as he is of the disease. You can be an instrument in his hand.

This may be the time appointed for the triumph that he wills over the disease that he ordained. Don't try to read the mind of God from his mysterious decrees of calamity. Do what he says: "Do good to everyone" (Galatians 6:10).

41

Does Anyone Standing by the Lake of Fire Jump In?

Reflections on How Willingly Sinners Enter Hell

C. S. Lewis is one of the top five dead people who have shaped the way I see and respond to the world. But he is not a reliable guide on a number of important theological matters. Hell is one of them.

His relentless stress was that people are not "sent" to hell but become their own hell. His emphasis was that we should think of "a bad man's perdition not as a sentence imposed on him but as the mere fact of being what he is."*

This inclines him to say, "All that are in hell choose it." And this leads some who follow Lewis in this emphasis to say things like, "All God does in the end with people is give them what they most want."

I come from the words of Jesus to this way of talking and find

---

*For all the relevant quotes, see Wayne Martindale and Jerry Root, eds., *The Quotable Lewis* (Carol Stream, IL: Tyndale, 1990), 288–95.

myself in a different world of discourse and sentiment. I think it is misleading to say that hell is giving people what they most want. I'm not saying you can't find a meaning for that statement that's true, perhaps in Romans 1:24–28. I'm saying that it's not a meaning that most people would give to it in light of what hell really is. I'm saying that the way Lewis dealt with hell and the way Jesus dealt with it are very different. And we would do well to follow Jesus.

The misery of hell will be so great that no one will want to be there. They will be weeping and gnashing their teeth (Matthew 8:12). Between their sobs, they will not speak the words, "I want this." They will not be able to say amid the flames of the lake of fire (Revelation 20:14), "I want this." "The smoke of their torment goes up forever and ever, and they have no rest, day or night" (Revelation 14:11). No one wants this.

When there are only two choices, and you choose against one, it does not mean that you want the other, if you are ignorant of the outcome of both. Unbelieving people know neither God nor hell. This ignorance is not innocent. Apart from regenerating grace, all people "by their unrighteousness suppress the truth" (Romans 1:18).

The person who rejects God does not know the real horrors of hell. This may be because he does not believe hell exists, or it may be because he convinces himself that it would be tolerably preferable to heaven.

But whatever he believes or does not believe, when he chooses against God, he is wrong about God and about hell. He is not, at that point, preferring the real hell over the real God. He is blind to both. He does not perceive the true glories of God, and he does not perceive the true horrors of hell.

So when a person chooses against God and, therefore, de facto chooses hell—or when he jokes about preferring hell with his friends over heaven with boring religious people—he does not know what he is doing. What he rejects is not the real heaven (nobody will be boring in heaven), and what he wants is not the real hell but the tolerable hell of his imagination.

When he dies, he will be shocked beyond words. The miseries are so great he would do anything in his power to escape. That it is not in his power to repent does not mean he wants to be there. Esau wept bitterly that he could not repent (Hebrews 12:17). The hell he was entering into he found to be totally miserable, and he wanted out. The meaning of hell is the scream, "I hate this, and I want out."

What sinners want is not hell but sin. That hell is the inevitable consequence of unforgiven sin does not mean people who choose sin want hell. It is not what people want—certainly not what they most want. Wanting sin is no more equal to wanting hell than wanting chocolate is equal to wanting obesity. Or wanting cigarettes is equal to wanting cancer.

Beneath this misleading emphasis on hell being what people "most want" is the notion that God does not "send" people to hell. But this is simply unbiblical. God certainly does send people to hell. He does pass sentence, and he executes it. Indeed, worse than that. God does not just *send*, he *throws*. "If anyone's name was not found written in the book of life, he was thrown (Greek, *eblethe*) into the lake of fire" (Revelation 20:15; see also Matthew 13:42; 25:30; Mark 9:47).

The reason the Bible speaks of people being "thrown" into hell is that no one will willingly go there, once they see what it really is. No one standing on the shore of the lake of fire jumps in. They do not choose it, and they will not want it. They have chosen sin. They have wanted sin. They do not want the punishment. When they come to the shore of this fiery lake, they must be thrown in.

When someone says that no one is in hell who doesn't want to be there, they give the false impression that hell is within the limits of what humans can tolerate. It inevitably gives the impression that hell is less horrible than Jesus says it is.

We should ask, How did Jesus expect his audience to think and feel about the way he spoke of hell? The words he chose were not chosen to soften the horror by being accommodating to cultural sensibilities. He spoke of a "fiery furnace" (Matthew 13:42) and "weeping and gnashing of teeth" (Luke 13:28) and "outer darkness" (Matthew 25:30) and "their worm [that] does not die" (Mark 9:48) and "eternal punishment" (Matthew 25:46) and "unquenchable fire" (Mark 9:43) and being "cut...in pieces" (Matthew 24:51).

These words are chosen to portray hell as an eternal, conscious experience that no one would or could ever want if they knew what they were choosing. Therefore, if someone is going to emphasize that people freely choose hell or that no one is there who doesn't want to be there, surely he should make every effort to clarify that, when they get there, they will *not* want this.

Surely the pattern of Jesus, who used blazing words to blast the hell-bent blindness out of everyone, should be followed. Surely, we will grope for words that show no one, no one, *no one* will *want* to be in hell when they experience what it really is. Surely everyone who desires to save people from hell will not mainly stress that it is "wantable" or "choosable," but that it is horrible beyond description: weeping, gnashing teeth, darkness, worm-eaten, fiery, furnacelike, dismembering, eternal, punishment, "an abhorrence to all flesh" (Isaiah 66:24).

As a hell-deserving sinner, I thank God for Jesus Christ my Savior, who became a curse for me and suffered hellish pain that he might deliver me from the wrath to come. While there is time, he will do that for anyone who turns from sin and treasures him and his work above all.

42

Stereotypes and Racism

Checking Ethnocentrism in Our
Statistical Generalizations

One of the serious challenges to freeing ourselves from ethnocentrism, or racism, is discerning when using a generalization is, in fact, the use of a stereotype. There is a difference. Life can't be lived without generalizations, as we will see, but they can be misused with great harm. Christians should want to get their cues on these things from God's Word, not the surrounding culture. In trying to think through these things, I came to three exhortations.

Exhortation #1: *Christians should not simply reflect the morality of their era but the morality of the Bible.*
The Bible says, "Do not be conformed to this world, but be transformed by the renewal of your mind" (Romans 12:2), and "Take no part in the unfruitful works of darkness, but instead expose them" (Ephesians 5:11).

Consider this quote from Shelby Steele's *White Guilt: How Blacks and Whites Together Destroyed the Promise of the Civil Rights Era.* As you read ask, How many Christians simply fit into the moral laxity of Eisenhower in his day and of Clinton in his day? Reflecting on the Clinton-Lewinsky sexual scandal compared to Dwight Eisenhower's reputed use of the N-word, Steele wrote:

> I wondered if President Clinton would be defended with relativism if he had done what, according to gossip, Eisenhower was said to have done. Suppose that in a light moment he had slipped into a parody of an old Arkansas buddy from childhood and, to get the voice right, used the word "nigger" a few times. Suppose further that a tape of this came to light so that all day long in the media—from the unctuous morning shows to the freewheeling late-night shows to the news every half hour on radio—we would hear the unmistakable presidential voice saying, "Take your average nigger...."
>
> A contribution of the civil rights movement was to establish the point that a multiracial society cannot be truly democratic unless social equality itself becomes a matter of *personal* morality. So a president's "immorality" in this area would pretty much cancel his legitimacy as a democratic leader.
>
> The point is that President Clinton survived what would certainly have destroyed President Eisenhower, and Eisenhower could easily have survived what would almost certainly have destroyed Clinton. Each man, finally, was no more than indiscreet within the moral landscape of his era (again, Eisenhower's indiscretion is hypothetical here for purposes of discussion). Neither racism in the fifties nor

womanizing in the nineties was a profound enough sin to undermine completely the moral authority of a president. So it was the good luck of each president to sin into the moral relativism of his era rather than into its Puritanism. And, interestingly, the moral relativism of one era was the Puritanism of the other. Race simply replaced sex as the primary focus of America's moral seriousness.*

This is the implication for Christians: Let the Bible, and not the era, govern our moral seriousness.

Exhortation #2: *Christians should not be guilty of stereotyping groups, recognizing that stereotyping is different from the just and loving use of generalization.*

The Bible says, "Do not judge by appearances, but judge with right judgment" (John 7:24).

In our ordinary use of language today, a stereotype is a generalization that is *not* built on what Jesus calls "right judgment." Merriam-Webster defines *stereotype* as a "standardized mental picture that is held in common by members of a group and that represents an *oversimplified* opinion, *prejudiced* attitude, or *uncritical* judgment."

This is the implication for Christians: Beware of forming stereotypes, or unjustified generalizations. Not only do they tend to hurt people (or unduly puff up the pride of others), but they are also unreliable guides in life.

---

*Shelby Steele, *White Guilt: How Blacks and Whites Together Destroyed the Promise of the Civil Rights Era* (New York: Harper, 2007), 5–6.

Exhortation #3: *Christians should use generalizations justly and lovingly to form true and helpful judgments about people and life.*

The Bible says, "So whatever you wish that others would do to you, do also to them, for this is the Law and the Prophets" (Matthew 7:12).

What is a generalization? A *generalization* is a general statement, law, principle, or proposition about a situation or a thing or a person or a group based on what we have generally observed from similar situations, things, persons, groups. Without them wise living is impossible.

- Many mushrooms are poisonous, and in general they have a certain spongy appearance. This generalization will keep you from experimenting with them in the woods when you are hungry and may save your life.

- Thin boards generally will not hold up a heavy man when stretched over wide spaces. This generalization will keep you from falling in the river.

- Generally, people in America stop when the light is red for them and green for you. You count on this and thus the traffic can keep flowing.

So the tough question is, When is a generalization about a group racist? I am using the word *racist* as something sinful, and the following answers move toward a definition. The following way of using a generalization would be wrong (racist):

- Using a generalization is wrong when you want a person to fit a negative generalization that you have formed about a group (even if the generalization statistically is true).

- Using a generalization is wrong when you assume that a statistically true negative generalization is true of a

particular person in the face of individual evidence to
the contrary.

- Using a generalization is wrong when you treat all the
  members of a group as if all must be characterized by a
  negative generalization.

- Using a generalization is wrong when you speak dispar-
  agingly of an entire group on the basis of a negative generalization without any regard for those in the group
  who don't fit the generalization. Or when you speak
  negatively of a group based on a generalization without
  giving any evidence that you acknowledge and appreciate the exceptions. (I assume that Jesus' generalizations
  about the Pharisees in Matthew 23 and Paul's generalization about the Cretans in Titus 1:12 are not sinful
  because they did have such regard and did appreciate
  the exceptions.)

This is the implication for Christians: While realizing that life is
not livable without generalizations, be careful not to let your pride
lead you to use statistical generalizations in unloving ways.

43

The Unbelieving Poet Catches a Glimpse of Truth

When Beauty Becomes Irresistible

Since all humans are created in the image of God (Genesis 1:27), and the work of God's law is written on every heart (Romans 2:15), and the heavens are telling the glory of God to everyone who can see (Psalm 19:1), and God has put eternity in man's heart (Ecclesiastes 3:11), and by God's providence every person is set to grope for God (Acts 17:27), and in God we all live and move and have our being (Acts 17:28), it is not surprising that even people without eyes to see the glory of Christ nevertheless have glimpses into the way the world really is, and then they don't know what to do with them.

Stephen Dunn is a Pulitzer Prize–winning poet and not a Christian. "I think of God as a metaphor. God is a metaphor for the origins and mysteries of the world.... I think of beliefs as provisional. They're not things that constitute anything fixed."

In an interview for *Books & Culture*, Aaron Rench asked him about his book *The Insistence of Beauty*.

RENCH: What is this notion that beauty has a demanding, compelling quality to it? Why is beauty that way?

DUNN: I just think beauty is irresistible. It disarms us. Takes away our arguments. And then if you expand the notion of beauty—that there is beauty in the tawdry, beauty in ugliness—things get complicated. But I think that beauty, which is more related in my mind to the sublime, is what we cannot resist.*

Yes, and this is how we all were converted to Christ. The eyes of our hearts were enlightened to see the beauty of Christ, and in that moment he became irresistible. This is the way divine, spiritual beauty works. It authenticates itself. It "takes away our arguments." Or better, it replaces all our false arguments with one grand, true argument that cannot be resisted.

This is the point Paul made: "The god of this world has blinded the minds of the unbelievers, to keep them from seeing the light of the gospel of the glory of Christ, who is the image of God" (2 Corinthians 4:4).

The "glory of Christ" is the beauty of Christ. It is the radiance of the fullness of his person—the impact of all his perfections. The reason people do not believe in Christ is that they do not see what is really there. That is what it means to be blind. Beauty is really there to be seen, but we are blind to it.

If we see it, we believe. "Beauty is irresistible." If you resist, you have not seen Christ as beautiful as he is (1 John 3:6). So the way we are converted to Christ is by having this blindness taken away. Scripture says, "[God] has shone in our hearts to give the light of the knowledge of the glory of God in the face of Jesus Christ" (2 Corinthians 4:6). God replaces blindness with light. The light is specifically "the glory of God in the face of Christ." It's the beauty of Christ.

That is all it takes. There is no coercion after that revelation. The light—the beauty—compels. We don't behold it and then ponder whether to believe. If we are still pondering, we have not yet seen.

Poet Stephen Dunn, groping toward God, says that beauty "is related to the sublime." It is "what we cannot resist." Yes, the sublime is summed up in Jesus Christ. And it is his glory that is supremely irresistible.

Let this be your life: Ponder him; be pervaded with him; point to him. The more you know of him and the more you admire the fullness of his beauty, the more you will reflect him. O that there would be thousands of irresistible reflections of the beauty of Jesus. May it be said of such reflections, "It disarms us. It takes away our arguments."

44

The Deceitful and Deadly Health-and-Wealth Teaching

Seven Pleas to Prosperity Preachers

When I read about prosperity-preaching churches, my response is, if I were not on the inside of Christianity, I would not want in. In other words, if this is the message of Jesus, no thank you.

Luring people to Christ to get rich is both deceitful and deadly. It's deceitful because when Jesus himself called us, he said things like, "Any one of you who does not renounce all that he has cannot be my disciple" (Luke 14:33). And it's deadly because the desire to be rich plunges "people into ruin and destruction" (1 Timothy 6:9). So here is my plea to preachers of the gospel.

1. Don't develop a philosophy of ministry that makes it harder for people to get into heaven.

Jesus said, "How difficult it will be for those who have wealth to enter the kingdom of God!" His disciples were astonished, as many in the "prosperity" movement should be. So Jesus went on to raise their astonishment even higher by saying, "It is easier for a camel to go through the eye of a needle than for a rich person to enter the kingdom of God." They responded in disbelief, "Then who can be saved?" Jesus said, "With man it is impossible, but not with God. For all things are possible with God" (Mark 10:23–27).

My question for prosperity preachers is, why would you want to develop a ministry focus that makes it harder for people to enter heaven?

2. Don't develop a philosophy of ministry that kindles suicidal desires in people.

Paul said, "Godliness with contentment is great gain, for we brought nothing into the world, and we cannot take anything out of the world. But if we have food and clothing, with these we will be content" (1 Timothy 6:6–8). But then he warned against the desire to be rich. And by implication, he warned against preachers who stir up the desire to be rich instead of helping people get rid of it. He warned, "Those who desire to be rich fall into temptation, into a snare, into many senseless and harmful desires that plunge people into ruin and destruction. For the love of money is a root of all kinds of evils. It is through this craving that some have wandered away from the faith and pierced themselves with many pangs" (1 Timothy 6:9–10).

So my question for prosperity preachers is, why would you want to develop a ministry that encourages people to pierce themselves with many pangs and plunge themselves into ruin and destruction?

3. Don't develop a philosophy of ministry that encourages vulnerability to moth and rust.

Jesus warned against the effort to lay up treasures on earth: "Do not lay up for yourselves treasures on earth, where moth and rust destroy and where thieves break in and steal, but lay up for yourselves treasures in heaven, where neither moth nor rust destroys and where thieves do not break in and steal" (Matthew 6:19–20). That is, we must be givers, not keepers.

Yes, we all keep something. But given the built-in tendency toward greed in all of us, why would we take the focus off Jesus and turn it upside down?

4. Don't develop a philosophy of ministry that makes hard work a means of amassing wealth.

Paul said we should not steal. The alternative is hard work with our own hands. But the main purpose is not merely to hoard or even to have. The purpose is to have to *give:* "Let him labor, doing honest work with his own hands, so that he may have something to share with anyone in need" (Ephesians 4:28). This is not a justification for being rich in order to give more. It is a call to make more and keep less so we can give more. There is no reason why a person who makes $200,000 should live any differently from the way a person who makes $80,000. Find a wartime lifestyle, cap your expenditures, and then give the rest away. It's not that simple. But that is the principle.

Why would you want to encourage people to think they should possess wealth in order to be a lavish giver? Why not encourage them to keep their lives more simple and be an even more lavish giver? Would that not add to their generosity a strong testimony that Christ, and not possessions, is their treasure?

5. Don't develop a philosophy of ministry that promotes less faith in the promises of God.

The reason the writer to the Hebrews tells us to be content with what we have is that being the opposite implies having less faith in the promises of God. He said, "Keep your life free from love of money, and be content with what you have, for he has said, 'I will never leave you nor forsake you.' So we can confidently say, 'The Lord is my helper; I will not fear; what can man do to me?'" (Hebrews 13:5–6).

If the Bible tells us that being content with what we have honors the promise of God never to forsake us, why would we want to teach people to want to be rich?

6. Don't develop a philosophy of ministry that contributes to your people being choked to death.

Jesus warned that the Word of God, which is meant to give us life, can be choked off from any effectiveness by riches. He said it is like a seed that grows up among thorns that choke it to death: "They are those who hear, but as they go on their way they are choked by the… riches…of life, and their fruit does not mature" (Luke 8:14).

Why would we want to encourage people to pursue the very thing that Jesus warned will choke us to death?

7. Don't develop a philosophy of ministry that takes the seasoning out of the salt and puts the light under a basket.

What is it about Christians that makes us the salt of the earth and the light of the world? It is not wealth. The desire for wealth and the pursuit of wealth tastes and looks just like the world. It does not offer the world anything different from what it already believes in. The great tragedy of prosperity preaching is that a person does not have to be spiritually awakened in order to embrace it; one needs only to be greedy. Getting rich in the name of Jesus is not the salt of the earth or the light of the world. In this, the world simply sees a reflection of itself. And if it works, they will buy it.

The context of Jesus' saying shows us what the salt and light are. They are the joyful willingness to suffer for Christ. Jesus said, "Blessed are you when others revile you and persecute you and utter all kinds of evil against you falsely on my account. Rejoice and be glad, for your reward is great in heaven, for so they persecuted the prophets who were before you. You are the salt of the earth.... You are the light of the world" (Matthew 5:11–14).

What will make the world taste (the salt) and see (the light) Christ in us is not that we love wealth the same way they do. Rather, it will be the willingness and the ability of Christians to love others through suffering, all the while rejoicing because their reward is in heaven with Jesus. This is inexplicable in human terms. This is supernatural. But to attract people with promises of prosperity is simply natural. It is not the message of Jesus. It is not what he died to achieve.

45

Sheep, Wolves, Snakes, and Doves

Thoughts on Matthew 10:16

Jesus said, "Behold, I am sending you out as sheep in the midst of wolves, so be wise as serpents and innocent as doves" (Matthew 10:16).

When Jesus sends us to bear witness to him in the world, he does not send us out as dominant and strong, but as weak and seemingly defenseless in ourselves. The only reason I say "seemingly" defenseless is that it is possible that, since all authority belongs to Jesus, he might intervene and shut the mouths of the wolves, like he did the mouths of the lions that surrounded Daniel.

But that does not appear to be his intention. The text goes on to say that the "wolves" will deliver the "sheep" to courts and flog them and drag them before governors and have parents and children put to death and hate them and persecute them from town to town and malign them and kill them (Matthew 10:17–31). So it is clear that when Jesus says he is sending us as sheep in the midst of wolves, he means that we will be treated the way wolves treat sheep.

But even though sheep are proverbially stupid—which, on the face of it, is what it looks like when they walk toward wolves and not away from them—Jesus countered that notion by saying "be wise as serpents." So vulnerability, not stupidity, is the point of calling us sheep. Be like snakes, not sheep, when it comes to being smart. I take that to mean that snakes are quick to get out of the way. They go under a rock.

So, yes, go among wolves and be vulnerable as you preach the gospel, but when they lunge at you, step aside. When they open their mouths, don't jump in. And not only that, be as innocent as doves. That is, don't give them any legitimate reason to accuse you of injustice or immorality. Keep your reputation as clean as you can.

So both the snakelike intelligence and the dovelike innocence are both designed to keep the sheep out of trouble. Jesus does not mean for us to get ourselves into as much difficulty as possible. He means to risk your lives as vulnerable, noncombative, sheeplike, courageous witnesses, but try to find ways to give your witness in a way that does not bring down unnecessary persecution.

This brings us to the dilemma that has faced many faithful witnesses: When do you flee from danger, and when do you embrace it and witness through it? In 1684, John Bunyan published a book called *Seasonable Counsel or Advice to Sufferers*. In it, he addressed this question: When does a sufferer flee (from danger) and when does he stand (and suffer the danger)? Bunyan knew how to answer for himself. He had four children, one of them blind, and he chose to remain in prison for twelve years rather than promise not to preach the gospel. How does he answer the question for others? May we try to escape?

Thou mayest do in this as it is in thy heart. If it is in thy heart to fly, fly; if it be in thy heart to stand, stand. Anything but a denial of the truth. He that flies, has warrant to do so; he that stands, has warrant to do so. Yea, the same man may both fly and stand, as the call and working of God with his heart may be. Moses fled, Exodus 2:15; Moses stood, Hebrews 11:27. David fled, 1 Samuel 19:12; David stood, 1 Samuel 24:8. Jeremiah fled, Jeremiah 37:11–12; Jeremiah stood, Jeremiah 38:17. Christ withdrew himself, Luke 9:10; Christ stood, John 18:1–8. Paul fled, 2 Corinthians 11:33; Paul stood, Acts 20:22–23.…

There are few rules in this case. The man himself is best able to judge concerning his present strength, and what weight this or that argument has upon his heart to stand or fly.… Do not fly out of a slavish fear, but rather because flying is an ordinance of God, opening a door for the escape of some, which door is opened by God's providence, and the escape countenanced by God's word, Matthew 10:23.…

If, therefore, when thou hast fled, thou art taken, be not offended at God or man: not at God, for thou art his servant, thy life and thy all are his; not at man, for he is but God's rod, and is ordained, in this, to do thee good. Hast thou escaped? Laugh. Art thou taken? Laugh. I mean, be pleased which [how] soever things shall go, for that the scales are still in God's hand.*

---

*John Bunyan, *Seasonable Counsels, or Advice to Sufferers,* in Works, Vol. 2, ed. George Offor (Edinburgh: The Banner of Truth Trust, 1991, reprinted from the 1854 edition published by W. G. Blackie and Son, Glasgow), 726.

Let us be slow to judge the missionary who chooses death rather than escape. And let us be slow to judge the missionary who chooses escape. Rather, let us give ourselves daily to the disciplines of Word saturation and obedience which transform us by the renewing of our minds that we may prove what is the will of God, what is good and acceptable and perfect in the moment of absolute urgency (Romans 12:2).

46

Abolition and the Roots of Public Justice

The Public Power of Protestant Justification

One of the most important and least known facts about the battle to abolish the slave trade in Britain two hundred years ago is that it was sustained by a passion for the doctrine of justification by faith alone. William Wilberforce was a spiritually exuberant and doctrinally rigorous evangelical. He battled tirelessly in Parliament for the outlawing of the British slave trade. It was doctrine that nourished the joy that sustained the battle that ended the vicious trade.

The key to understanding Wilberforce is to read his own book, *A Practical View of Christianity*. It's the only book he wrote. There he argued that the fatal habit of his day was to separate Christian morals from Christian doctrines. His conviction was that there is "perfect harmony between the leading doctrines and the practical precepts of Christianity." He had seen the devastating effects of denying this: "The peculiar doctrines of Christianity went more and more out of sight, and…the moral system itself also began to wither and decay, being robbed of that which should have supplied it with life and nutriment." But Wilberforce knew that "the whole superstructure of Christian morals is grounded on their deep and ample basis."

This "ample basis" and these "peculiar doctrines" that sustained Wilberforce in the battle against the slave trade were the doctrines of human depravity, divine judgment, the substitutionary work of Christ on the cross, justification by faith alone, regeneration by the Holy Spirit, and the practical necessity of fruit in a life devoted to good deeds. Wilberforce was not a political pragmatist. He was a radically God-centered, Christian politician. And his zeal for Christ, rooted in these "peculiar doctrines," was the strength that sustained him in the battle.

At the center of these essential "gigantic truths" was (and is) justification by faith alone. The indomitable joy that perseveres in the battle for justice is grounded in the experience of Jesus Christ as our righteousness. "If we would…rejoice," Wilberforce said, "as triumphantly as the first Christians did; we must learn, like them to repose our entire trust in [Christ] and to adopt the language of the apostle, 'God forbid that I should glory, save in the cross of Jesus Christ,' 'who of God is made unto us wisdom and righteousness, and sanctification, and redemption.'"

In other words, the doctrine of justification is essential to right living—and that includes political living. Astonishingly, Wilberforce said that the spiritual and practical errors of his day that gave strength to the slave trade were owing to the failure to experience the truth of this doctrine:

> They consider not that Christianity is a scheme "for justifying the ungodly" by Christ's dying for them "when yet sinners"—

a scheme "for reconciling us to God"—when enemies; and for making the fruits of holiness the effects, not the cause, of our being justified and reconciled.

This was why he wrote *A Practical View of Christianity.* The "bulk" of Christians in his day, he observed, were "nominal"—that is, they pursued morality without first relying utterly on the free gift of justification by grace alone through faith alone on the basis of Christ alone. They got things backward. First they strived for moral uplift, and then they appealed to God for approval. That is not the Christian gospel. And it will not transform a nation. It would not sustain a politician through eleven parliamentary defeats over twenty years of vitriolic opposition.

The battle for abolition was sustained by getting the gospel right: "The true Christian…knows…that this holiness is not to precede his reconciliation to God, and be its cause; but to follow it, and be its effect. That, in short, it is by faith in Christ only that he is to be justified in the sight of God." When Wilberforce put things in this order, he found invincible strength and courage to stand for the justice of abolition.

When we call to mind the abolition of the British slave trade, may Jesus Christ, the righteous One, receive the credit he is due in the life of William Wilberforce.

47

Topple Every Idol

*Fighting Covetousness
by Looking at Others*

Achan stole and lied (Joshua 7:11). Jericho had fallen before
Israel. The riches of the city were not to be taken, but Achan
took garments and silver and gold. He hid them and tried to deceive
the leaders.

Why did he do that? When he was caught, Achan gave the answer: "I *coveted* them and took them" (Joshua 7:21). Covetousness.
He *desired* the silver, gold, and garments more than he desired fellowship with God.

There is no difference between the Hebrew word for "desire" and
the Hebrew word for "covet." Coveting means "desiring something
too much." And too much is measured by how that desiring compares
to desiring God. If desiring leads you away from God rather than
closer to God, it is covetousness. It is sin.

I suspect that the reason the Ten Commandments began with
the commandment "You shall have no other gods before me" (Exodus
20:3) and ends with the commandment "You shall not covet" (Exodus 20:17) is that they are essentially the same commandment, one

focusing on what we should desire (God) and one focusing on what we shouldn't (anything else more than God). They bracket the other eight commandments and reveal their source.

Not coveting means not desiring anything in a way that diminishes God as your supreme treasure. And not having any gods before God means the same thing: Don't treasure anything or anyone in a way that competes with God's supreme place in your life. Idolatry is what we call disobedience to the first commandment. And idolatry is what Paul called disobedience to the tenth commandment ("covetousness, which is idolatry," Colossians 3:5).

So Achan stole and lied because God was not his supreme treasure. He was not satisfied in all that God promised to be for him. That is probably why Joshua said to Achan when he was found out, "My son, give glory to the LORD God" (Joshua 7:19). It demeans the glory of God when we prefer anything above him. That was Achan's chief sin. Desiring gold more than God equals covetousness, which equals idolatry, which demeans God.

How can we keep our lives free from this dreadful condition— desiring other things more than God, coveting, being idolaters? One answer is the Word of God: "I have stored up your word in my heart, that I might not sin against you" (Psalm 119:11).

Another answer comes from Philippians. Paul described the condition we all want to be in. He said, "Whatever gain I had, I counted as loss for the sake of Christ. Indeed, I count everything as loss because of the surpassing worth of knowing Christ Jesus my Lord" (Philippians 3:7–8). That is exactly the opposite of covetousness. That is the opposite of idolatry. That is supreme satisfaction in Christ. That is freedom.

Does Paul have a practical suggestion that we can use to fight for this satisfaction in Christ? Yes, he does: "Brothers, join in imitating me, *and* keep your eyes on those who walk according to the example you have in us" (Philippians 3:17).

I have some amazingly practical help for us. Pick out some people whose lives show that they treasure Christ above other things. Then keep your eyes on them, as Paul said. Watch them. That is a good way to conquer covetousness.

There are some folks whose maturity and wisdom and spiritual fruitfulness in their marriages, for example, is so admirable that I look at them and think about them a lot. When I am struggling with what I should feel and do in my marriage, I think about what they would do. I think Paul meant something like that.

I would only add that it is good to have some dead saints to "keep your eyes on" as well. That's what Christian biographies are for.

So flee covetousness. Topple all your idols. "Count everything as loss because of the surpassing worth of knowing Christ." Be in the Word every day. But also find those who live this way and "keep your eyes on them." What you will see, if you look carefully, is the power and beauty of Christ. This sight will satisfy your soul. And your satisfied soul will keep you from coveting (and lying and stealing like Achan). And your life will make God look supremely valuable.

48

Creating Pointers to the Greatness of Christ

Why and How I Tweet

I see two kinds of responses to social media like blogging, Facebook, Twitter, and others.

One says: These media tend to shorten attention spans, weaken discursive reasoning, lure people away from Scripture and prayer, disembody relationships, feed the fires of narcissism, cater to the craving for attention, fill the world with drivel, shrink the soul's capacity for greatness, and make us second-handers who comment on life when we ought to be living it. So boycott them and write books (not blogs) about the problem.

The second response says: Yes, there is truth in all that, but instead of boycotting, try to fill these media with as much provocative, reasonable, Bible-saturated, prayerful, relational, Christ-exalting, truth-driven, serious, creative pointers to true greatness as you can.

I lean toward the second response. *Lean* is different from *leap*. We are aware that the medium tends to shape the message. This has been true, more or less, with every new medium that has come along—speech, drawing, handwriting, print, books, magazines, newspapers, tracts, 16mm home movies, flannelgraph, Cinerama, movies, Gospel Blimps, TV, radio, cassette tapes, 8-tracks, blackboards, whiteboards, overhead projection, PowerPoint, skits, drama, banners, CDs, MP3s, DVDs, skywriting, video, texting, blogging, tweeting, mynah bird training, etc.

Danger, danger everywhere. Yes. But it seems to us that aggressive efforts to saturate media with the supremacy of God, the truth of Scripture, the glory of Christ, the joy of the gospel, the insanity of sin, and the radical nature of Christian living is a good choice for some Christians. Not all. Everyone should abstain from some of these media. For example, the Pipers don't have a television.

That's my general disposition toward media.

Now what about Twitter? I find Twitter to be a kind of taunt: "Okay, truth-lover, see what you can do with 140 characters! You say your mission is to spread a passion for the supremacy of God in all things! Well, this is one of those 'all things.' Can you magnify Christ with this thimbleful of letters?"

To which I respond:

> The sovereign Lord of the earth and sky
> Puts camels through a needle's eye.
> And if his wisdom judge it mete,
> He will put worlds inside a tweet.

It also seems to be that the book of Proverbs is God's Twitter compilation for us. So when I think about my life goal and when I think about how God uses proverbs, I am not inclined to tweet that at 10 a.m. the cat pulled the curtains down. But I am inclined to tweet: The Lion of Judah will roll up the sky like a scroll and put the sun out with his brighter glory (128 characters). If God answers my prayer, that tweet might distract someone from pornography and make him look up to something greater.

In spite of all the dangers, Twitter seemed like a risk worth taking. "All things were created through [Christ] and for [Christ]" (Colossians 1:16). The world does not know it, but that is why Twitter exists and that's why I tweet.

49

What Will the Final Judgment Mean for You?

Thoughts on the Book of Life and Union with Christ

I am writing this on New Year's Eve. The ending of another year moves my mind to other endings—like the final judgment. Ponder with me, if you wish, what it will be like to go through the last great judgment. It is good to settle in our minds what it will be like. If we could see it clearly now, it would make those who trust Christ the happiest and bravest people in the days ahead.

I do believe we will all face a final judgment with the rest of the world. "We will all stand before the judgment seat of God" (Romans 14:10; see also 2 Corinthians 5:10). When Jesus said, "Whoever hears my word and believes him who sent me has eternal life. *He does not come into judgment,* but has passed from death to life" (John 5:24), I take him to mean that we will not be condemned in the final judgment because our sentence has already been passed—not guilty. So why are we there at the last judgment?

John paints us a picture in Revelation:

I saw the dead, great and small, standing before the throne, and books were opened. Then another book was opened, which is the book of life. And the dead were judged by what was written in the books, according to what they had done. And the sea gave up the dead who were in it, Death and Hades gave up the dead who were in them, and they were judged, each one of them, according to what they had done. Then Death and Hades were thrown into the lake of fire. This is the second death, the lake of fire. And if anyone's name was not found written in the book of life, he was thrown into the lake of fire. (Revelation 20:12–15)

There are books (v. 12), and there is a book (vv. 12, 15). The book is called "the book of life." The books record the deeds of all people (including ours). This is implied when John said, "The dead were judged by what was written in the *books, according to what they had done*…and they were judged, each one of them, *according to what they had done*" (vv. 12–13).

All the dead are judged in view of what is written in the books. This includes believers and unbelievers, elect and nonelect. This is a judgment of all people: "I saw the dead, great and small" (v. 12). "The dead were judged" (v. 12). "The sea gave up the dead who were in it, Death and Hades gave up the dead who were in them, and they were judged" (v. 13). So believers and unbelievers face what is written in the books. It matters. But how does it matter?

To answer that, we need to see what it means to have your name written in the book of life (vv. 12, 15). In Revelation 13:8, John said, "All who dwell on earth will worship [the beast], everyone whose name has not been written before the foundation of the world in the book of life of the Lamb who was slain." Two things are crucial here:

- The names have been in the book of life since before Creation. So this is a reference to the elect (Revelation 3:5)—those who would certainly believe on Christ and be saved through him.

- A name written in the book of life ensures that a person will not worship the beast. This is implied in saying everyone will worship the beast *except* those whose names are written in the book of life. If your name is in the book of life, you will not worship the beast. That is not a coincidence. Being in the book means belonging to God, who keeps his elect from demon worship. John said the same thing again in chapter 17: "The dwellers on earth whose names have not been written in the book of life from the foundation of the world will marvel to see the beast" (Revelation 17:8). Being in the book ensures that you will not marvel at the beast. It means God will keep you. You will persevere and be saved.

So we come back to the judgment in Revelation 20. "If anyone's name was not found written in the book of life, he was thrown into the lake of fire" (v. 15). This implies that being in the book of life ensures that one will not perish. Salvation is secured for all who are written in the book of life.

The reason that being written in the book of life secures our salvation is that the book is called "the book of life of the Lamb who was slain" (Revelation 13:8). The names in this book are not saved on the basis of their deeds. They are saved on the basis of Christ's being slain. He "loves us and has freed us from our sins by his blood" (Revelation 1:5). We have been ransomed by his blood (Revelation 5:9).

So how then does the record of our lives contained in "the books" have a part in our judgment? The answer is that the books contain enough evidence of our belonging to Christ that they function as a public confirmation of our faith and our union with him. Consider this passage: "Nothing unclean will ever enter [the New Jerusalem], nor anyone who does what is detestable or false, but only those who are written in the Lamb's book of life" (Revelation 21:27).

Here the result of "being written in the book of life" is not only not perishing but also not making a practice of detestable, sinful behaviors. In other words, just as in Revelation 13:8, where being in the book of life ensures that one will not worship the beast, so in Revelation 21:27, being in the book of life ensures that one will not make a practice of detestable deeds.

Therefore, our deeds confirm that our names are in the book and should be in the book—that is, they confirm that we trust Christ and are united with him. Our deeds are the fruit of our faith and union with Christ.

For example, consider the thief on the cross. Jesus said that he would enter paradise (Luke 23:43). But what will judgment be like for him when the books are opened? I believe 99.9 percent of his life will be sin, because whatever is not from faith is sin (Romans 14:23). Only the final minutes of his life on the cross will be the fruit of faith. I think God will open the book of life and show the name of the thief on the cross. His salvation will be secured by the blood of Christ.

Then God will open the books and will use the record of sin to glorify his Son's supreme sacrifice, and then he will use the last page to show the change that was wrought in the thief's attitudes and words. That last page—the last hours on the cross—will be the public confirmation of the thief's faith and union with Christ.

Therefore, when I say that what is written in the books is a public confirmation of our faith and of union with Christ, I do not mean that the record will contain more good works than bad works. I mean that there will be recorded there the practical evidences that show the reality of faith—the reality of regeneration and union with Christ. There will be enough evidences of grace that God will be able to make a public display of what is in the books to verify the born-again reality of those written in the book of life.

No one is saved on the basis of his works. But everyone who is saved does new works. Not perfectly but with humble longing for more holiness. That is how I face today and tomorrow, confident that my condemnation is past (Romans 8:3), that my name is in the book of life, and that the One who began a good work in me will bring it to completion at the day of Christ. I pray for you, that you are with me in this confidence.

Let's Make Some Resolutions

*Endeavoring Fresh Good for
the Glory of God*

God approves of New Year's resolutions. And midyear and three-quarters-year and monthly and weekly and daily resolutions. Any and all resolutions for good have God's approval—*if* we resolve by faith in Jesus.

I would like to encourage you to make some resolutions. Socrates said, "The unexamined life is not worth living." Well, the examined life is not worth living either if the examination produces no resolutions. What examination and experience teach us is that the unplanned life settles into fruitless routine. The drifting life—the coasting, *que sera sera* unreflective life—tends to be a wasted life.

The opposite of this is self-examination—life examination, routine examination, schedule examination, heart examination—followed by "resolves for good." That's what I encourage you to do. Here's why I think God will be pleased when you do this by faith in Jesus.

Paul said to the Thessalonians:

To this end we always pray for you, that our God may make
you worthy of his calling and may fulfill every resolve for good
and every work of faith by his power, so that the name of our
Lord Jesus may be glorified in you, and you in him, according
to the grace of our God and the Lord Jesus Christ. (2 Thessalonians 1:11–12)

I find this extremely encouraging. Paul prays for us, and I pray for
you even as I write this, that God will "fulfill every resolve for good"
that we have. This means that it is good to have resolves. God approves of it. It also means that our resolving is important, but that
God's enabling us to fulfill the resolves is crucial. Paul wouldn't pray
if God's help weren't needed. "The heart of man plans [resolves!] his
way, but the LORD establishes [fulfills!] his steps" (Proverbs 16:9).

But it matters how we resolve. When Paul said, "Every resolve for
good and every work of faith," he was not describing two different
acts. He was describing one act in two ways. It is a "resolve for good"
because we will it. It is a "work of faith" because we depend on Jesus
to give us power to fulfill it. That's how we resolve. It's by faith in
Jesus.

So Paul said that the fulfilling of the resolve is "by his power."
That's what we are depending on. That's what we are looking for
when we resolve. We are looking to Jesus, who promised to be with us
and help us. "I know that through…the help of the Spirit of Jesus
Christ this will turn out for my deliverance" (Philippians 1:19).

This explains the words "so that" in Paul's prayer: "*So that* the name of our Lord Jesus may be glorified in you" (2 Thessalonians 1:12). When you resolve something good and trust in the power of Jesus to help you do it, then "the name of our Lord Jesus is glorified." If you depend on *your* willpower, *your* name will be glorified. The giver gets the glory.

So Christian resolutions are different from the world's resolutions. We believe that by grace alone we have been called—that is, captured by the truth and beauty of Christ. We resolve things not to make God be for us, but because he is already for us—that's what his call makes plain. He opens our eyes to see and trust Christ. He shows us, in the cross, that he is totally for us. All our resolves are to walk more worthy of this calling, in ways more fitting for the beneficiaries of such free grace.

They are faith resolves—faith that we are loved and called and justified. And faith that, therefore, Jesus will help us do what we resolve to do. When we resolve like that, the name of our Lord Jesus is magnified.

So sometime soon pause and examine your life. Examine what is missing that should be there. What is there that should be removed? What new dreams for ministry might you venture? What new habits do you want to build into your schedule?

Remember, God will be pleased with new resolves for good if you resolve *by faith in Jesus*. I am praying for you "that our God may make you worthy of his calling and may fulfill every resolve for good and every work of faith by his power" (2 Thessalonians 1:11).

A NOTE ON RESOURCES

desiringGod

If you would like to explore further the vision of God and life presented in this book, we at Desiring God would love to serve you. We have thousands of resources to help you grow in your passion for Jesus Christ and help you spread that passion to others. At desiringGod.org, you'll find almost everything John Piper has written and preached, including more than sixty books. We've made over thirty years of his sermons available free online for you to read, listen to, download, and watch.

In addition, you can access hundreds of articles, find out where John Piper is speaking, and learn about our conferences. Desiring God has a whatever-you-can-afford policy, designed for individuals with limited discretionary funds. If you'd like more information about this policy, please contact us at the address or phone number below. We exist to help you treasure Jesus and his gospel above all things because *he is most glorified in you when you are most satisfied in him.* Let us know how we can serve you!

Desiring God

Post Office Box 2901 / Minneapolis, Minnesota 55402
888.346.4700 mail@desiringGod.org

Delight in God is not optional.
It's essential

Some call it "the Piper trilogy." *Desiring God*,
The Pleasures of God, and *Future Grace*
represent the heart and fabric of John Piper's
theology — which rises as high as God's eternal
nature, goes as deep as our unavoidable ache
to be happy, and gets as practical as
the everyday Christian life.

DVDs and Study Guides available separately.

WaterBrook Multnomah
Publishing Group

Taste and see how good God is.

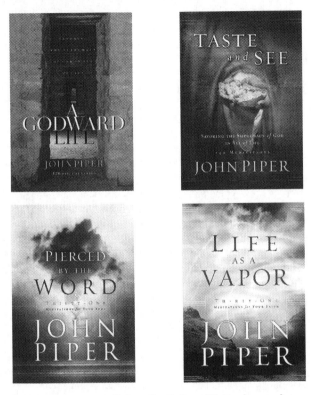

This is true soul food. John Piper's series of devotional meditations are steeped in the Bible, grown in the soil of pastoral ministry, and particularly crafted to nourish the hungry heart. Now, more than 365 individual readings are available in this series.

Printed in the United States
by Baker & Taylor Publisher Services